MAGNIFICENT SEVEN

THE CHAMPIONSHIP GAMES THAT BUILT THE LOMBARDI DYNASTY

PHOTOGRAPHS BY VERNON BIEVER AND JOHN BIEVER | TEXT BY BUD LEA

PAUL HORNUNG
Foreword

BART STARR
Introduction

VINCE LOMBARDI JR.
Afterword

TRIUMPH
BOOKS
CHICAGO

Library of Congress Cataloging-in-Publication Data

Lea, Bud.
    Magnificent seven : the championship games that built the Lombardi era / Bud Lea ; photographs by Vernon Biever and John Biever.
         p.   cm.
    Includes bibliographical references and index.
    ISBN 1-57243-476-7
      1. Green Bay Packers (Football team)—History.
    2. Lombardi, Vince. I. Title: the championship games that built the Lombardi era. II. Title.

GV956.G7 L43 2002
796.332′64′0974—dc21

2002019407

This book is available in quantity at special discounts for your group or organization. For further information, contact:
Triumph Books
601 South LaSalle Street
Suite 500
Chicago, Illinois, 60605
(312) 939-3330
Fax (312) 663-3557

Printed in the United States of America
ISBN 1-57243-476-7

CONTENTS

FOREWORD

When Vince Lombardi came to Green Bay to coach the Packers in 1959, everybody said, "Well, guys, we're going to be winners now." Although it was true, us saying so was a lot of hogwash. It was as if we knew all about Lombardi, when the fact was, we knew little if anything about him. He had been an assistant coach with the New York Giants and an assistant at Army, and this was his first job as a head coach.

From day one at Green Bay, we learned that things would never be the same.

I was the bonus choice of the 1957 National Football League draft—the first player selected—and after the Packers picked me they didn't know what to do with me. Coach Liz Blackbourn tried me at quarterback, at halfback, at fullback, and all but gave up on me. It was the same way with Scooter McLean, who followed Blackbourn.

After two frustrating and losing years, including the worst record (1–11–1) in Green Bay history, I was ready to quit pro football. I had a nice little real estate business with my uncle back home in Kentucky. We were doing quite well. I didn't need the Packers. I didn't want to be playing up there with a bunch of guys who didn't give a crap. Then, with the coaching change, I figured I'd give it another shot.

Lombardi got our attention immediately. He told us if we didn't give him 100 percent all the time our butts would be out of Green Bay. He laid down his rules right away.

That's what all of us needed. That's what I needed. From high school through college, I had coaches who bitched at me. That never bothered me. Lombardi bitched at everyone. He was tough, tougher than any coach I had ever known. But when he talked to us, he was direct and firm, and I started to want to play the game again.

He told me that I was going to be his halfback—not quarterback or fullback but halfback. I had one position to focus on, and I was determined to make the best of it.

Finally, I had a coach at Green Bay who knew how to coach. We knew he was going to be a very serious coach after our first meeting with him. That's the first thing I remember about him, how serious he was. I knew that things were going to change for the better.

For eight years, Vince Lombardi was the most important man in my life. I respected him as a coach, a leader, and, more important, as a friend. If I needed advice, I could talk to him. He was tougher on me than he was on most of the other players, but I needed that extra push.

I was very close to Lombardi, and the other players knew that. Whenever there was a problem on the team, the guys wanted me to go in and talk to him. They knew I could do this. But I never won an argument with him.

Like curfew. I went in there one summer at St. Norbert College and told him, "Damn it, the married guys get to go home on weekends to sleep with their wives, and the single guys are stuck in the dorms." I told him I was 29 years old and I had to get out of the dorm. He didn't change his rules. The single guys had to stay in the dorm during training camp.

The toughest time of my life came in 1963, when Pete Rozelle told me to come to New York. He said he wanted to talk to me privately and that it was very important. The commissioner told me the league was investigating me because of my betting habits. He told me he wanted me to keep this meeting with him in strictest confidence, which I did. Three months later, Rozelle announced that he was suspending me for betting on football games.

One of my big regrets about that whole mess was that I waited until the last moment to tell Lombardi. I told him that I was called to New York and had talked to the FBI and all those other people and that I had promised Rozelle that I wouldn't talk to anybody about the meeting or what he was going to do about me. Vince said he was really disappointed that I didn't call him. He said if I had called him, he could have helped me. I made a horrible mistake not calling Lombardi earlier.

After the 1967 season Lombardi put me on the expansion list, and the New Orleans Saints claimed me. He told me he didn't want to put me on that list, and he said he didn't think the Saints were going to take me because of my injuries. I *wanted* them to take me. I wanted to go down to New Orleans with Tom Fears as coach and get $350,000. That was a hell of a lot more money than I would be making in Green Bay.

I had hurt my neck during my last year with the Packers, and when I went down to New Orleans and underwent further medical tests, they said I couldn't play anymore. They told me I could end up a paraplegic if I got hit the right way. I never played one game for the Saints, and I worked out a contract deal with them. I took half of it and did radio and TV in New Orleans. I had a good year. Then I took a job in Chicago, doing the 6:00 and 10:00 sportscasts on WBBM, Channel 2.

When Lombardi left Green Bay to take over as coach of the Washington Redskins, he turned another losing team into a winner. Before the last home game he coached for the Redskins, he invited Max McGee and me to Washington. He wanted us to spend the weekend with him. He wanted us to stay at his house. I told him I didn't want that arrangement because I had lived through too many curfews with him. We told him to get us a hotel suite and a good one. He got us two suites at the best hotel downtown. He had a limo pick us up, and I told him we should have had this treatment when we were in Green Bay. He didn't laugh.

We went to dinner on Friday night. He took us to a fancy restaurant, and everybody in the place gave him a standing ovation when he walked in. I told him he had planned this whole thing and that he did it to show Max and me how well he had been received in the nation's capital. He got real embarrassed and then told both of us to shut up and enjoy the evening.

He beat the Saints on Sunday, and after the game Max and I went back to his house. He had Chief Justice Earl Warren over there, and he had Edward Bennett Williams, he had Barbara Walters—all these people were stopping by and having a drink.

And he didn't have a bartender, and I told him, how cheap can you be? He said, "What do you need a bartender for? Anybody can make a drink." So I told him to make me a little scotch on the rocks. He told me to make it myself. Finally, he had Ockie Krueger, an old friend from Army, making drinks for everyone.

When coach Lombardi became seriously ill and entered a hospital, I went to see him. Marie Lombardi warned me that I would be shocked when I saw him, and I was. He had lost 100 pounds and was very weak.

But he still had a lot of fight in him. He said he was going to beat the cancer. He said he would be back coaching the next year. I told him, "You bet your ass you will." I told him I had talked to Sonny Jurgensen and that they were all excited about winning it all next year. He died about two weeks after my visit.

Lombardi's years with the Packers are still among the greatest achievements in sports. Five NFL championships and victories in the first two Super Bowls are standards nobody else has reached. He is a legend, the best example of a winner we have in America. I believe he would have been a great commissioner for the NFL.

I loved every minute I spent with him. He was a very special man.

I'm very happy that Bud Lea has dedicated his time to write about the events that climaxed in the Packers winning seven championship games. I met Bud when the Packers drafted me out of Notre Dame. He wrote about us during the bad years and the best.

Lombardi disliked most sportswriters. He liked Bud. He thought Bud was fair. When Bud said Lombardi yelled at him as much as he did at the other reporters, I told him that just showed how much he liked him.

I've also known Vernon Biever for a long time. He's got the best picture ever taken of Vince and me. It's a black and white picture taken from the sidelines. I use it when I'm asked to charity events.

There have been many books written about Vince Lombardi, but this one is different. Bud Lea and Vernon Biever have combined their talents to make these championship games come to life.

It was a time in my life I will treasure forever.

—Paul Hornung
Louisville, Kentucky

ACKNOWLEDGMENTS

A major share of the information for this book came from personal interviews with the men who played and worked for Vince Lombardi's Green Bay Packers, a team the author covered for the *Milwaukee Sentinel*.

Those interviewed included Donny Anderson, Don Chandler, Red Cochran, Willie Davis, Boyd Dowler, Gale Gillingham, Forrest Gregg, Paul Hornung, Jerry Kramer, Chuck Lane, Bob Long, Max McGee, Chuck Mercein, Pat Peppler, Dave Robinson, Bob Skoronski, Bart Starr, Jim Taylor, and Fuzzy Thurston.

Much of the research was done through the *Milwaukee Sentinel*, *Milwaukee Journal*, *Green Bay Press-Gazette*, the Green Bay Packer Yearbook, and *Sports Illustrated*.

Other sources of information included:

Blair, Sam. *Dallas Cowboys: Pro or Con?* New York: Doubleday and Co., 1970.

Klein, Dave. *The Vince Lombardi Story.* New York: Lion Books, 1971.

Kramer, Jerry, and Dick Schaap. *Instant Replay.* New York: The World Publishing Co., 1968.

Maraniss, David. *When Pride Still Mattered.* New York: Simon and Schuster, 1999.

The National Football League. *Lombardi.* Chicago: Follett Publishing Co., 1971.

O'Brien, Michael. *Vince: A Personal Biography of Vince Lombardi.* New York: William Morrow & Co., 1987.

Perkins, Steve. *Next Year's Champions*. New York: The World Publishing Co, 1969.

Ralbovsky, Marty. *Super Bowl*. New York: Hawthorn Books, Inc., 1972.

The Super Bowl. New York: Simon and Schuster, 1990.

Wells, Robert. *Lombardi: His Life and Times*. Madison, WI: Wisconsin House, Ltd., 1971.

INTRODUCTION

What do you think of when you hear the title *The Magnificent Seven*? For those of you who happen to be movie fans, you may recall a terrific film starring Yul Brynner. In this story, Mr. Brynner plays the leader of a group of men who rescue a small town from a gang of outlaws. You probably know the outcome . . . the good guys won. As entertaining as this movie turned out to be, it was fiction. What the Green Bay Packers accomplished in their own "magnificent seven" was real. Like all great victories, these had their roots in humble beginnings.

The seeds for the seven championship games reviewed in this outstanding book were planted in 1959 when the Packers hired coach Vince Lombardi. I will never forget the first meeting he had with us. Remember, we had a poor record prior to his arrival, and we were probably no more confident than the citizens who needed Yul Brynner's help in the movie. All that began to change at that meeting. Coach Lombardi said, "We are going to relentlessly chase perfection, knowing full well that we will not achieve it, because perfection is not attainable. However, we are going to relentlessly pursue it because in the process we will achieve excellence." Then he paused. "I am not remotely interested," he continued, "in just being good." About 40 minutes into the meeting we took a break and I ran downstairs to the lobby of the Packer headquarters to call my wife on a pay phone. All I said to her was, "Honey, we're going to begin to win." And that's exactly what happened.

The following year, 1960, we made it to the NFL Championship game in Philadelphia despite our youth. We lost a hard fought battle, 17–13, just a few yards from a winning touchdown as time expired. Afterward we wondered if coach Lombardi would tear into us for coming so close but not closing the deal. Instead, he saluted us for our effort and told us that great things were in store for us. Then he concluded with a statement I'll always remember. "Gentlemen," he said, "Never again will we fail to win a championship game." From that point forward we played in seven of them, and were magnificent in every one.

I will not go into the details of each game because the gentlemen who have compiled this marvelous collection—my friends Bud Lea and Vern Biever—have already done so. However, I would like to share with you some of the key elements of our success, most of which are attributable to coach Lombardi. We learned about leadership in our first championship season, 1961. Coach Lombardi continually reminded us of our priorities, which he had strongly emphasized since arriving in Green Bay. Those priorities were God, our families, and the Green Bay Packers, in that order. That allowed us to keep our focus on what was truly important, and we moved our overall performance from very good to dominant by the end of the year.

We repeated our 1961 triumph over the Giants by defeating them in a rematch the following year. Not many fans remember this, but in those days the NFL simply rotated years to determine who would host the championship game. In even numbered years, the Eastern Conference Champion hosted the game, which meant that we had to travel to New York despite the facts that our record was 13–1 and many observers believed we had one of the best teams in history. Coach Lombardi reminded us traveling to New York was no obstacle to a team with the desire to repeat as champions as its goal. Despite the brutal winter weather, we never wavered and brought home the trophy to thousands of supportive fans in Green Bay.

After two winning but less-than-stellar campaigns in 1963 and 1964, coach Lombardi returned more energized than ever. This was when we truly learned the meaning of love for our team and teammates. That may sound like an unusual term to associate with Lombardi, but consider this quote from Cullen Hightower: "Love is what's left of a relationship after all the selfishness has been removed." Although Coach always taught us to put the team ahead of individuals, we had an even greater emphasis on this than usual, and the result was another championship. One of my best friends, Zeke Bratkowski, epitomized this. A very talented quarterback for many years, he was always filled with a positive attitude and was prepared to step in when called upon. Several times in 1965, both during the regular season and the playoffs, he had to perform in clutch situations after I sustained injuries. He was outstanding every time. This type of unselfishness, which ran through our veins, brought us our third championship of the sixties, a victory over Cleveland.

Packer fans everywhere are probably most familiar with the 1966 and 1967 years, in which we defeated the Cowboys and then went on to capture the first two Super Bowl titles. More than three decades later, coach Lombardi is often misquoted as saying "Winning isn't everything. It's the only thing." What he actually said was that winning isn't everything, but making the *effort* to win is. It's the willingness to prepare to win and give your best effort that is paramount. We had to do so during those years, because the Cowboys, the Chiefs, and the Raiders were all young, hungry, and talented teams. I am convinced that we could never have achieved the final components that went into our magnificent seven victories without coach Lombardi's wisdom and teaching regarding the willingness to prepare to win. Our unselfish love for each other, our focus, and our gratitude for the opportunity to play for such a magnificent leader resulted in a decade that has never been matched in NFL history.

I salute Bud Lea and Vern Biever for this memorable collection of stories and photographs that capture the glory of the magnificent seven. I hope you enjoy reading this book as much as I have.

—Bart Starr
Birmingham, Alabama

Paul Hornung spent his weekend furlough from the army in Green Bay by testing his throwing arm; Giants' tackle Dick Modzelewski couldn't reach him. Although he didn't complete a pass, Hornung proved to be too tough for the Giants to handle as he ran for 89 yards in 20 carries, caught three passes for 47 yards, scored a touchdown on a six-yard run, kicked three field goals, and added four extra points.

CHAPTER 1

THE 1961 NFL CHAMPIONSHIP GAME

They waited 28 years for this day. They waited through four coaching changes and hundreds of players. They waited through years of hearing they weren't big enough to play host to a National Football League championship game.

Curly Lambeau, who helped found the team in 1919, had coached the Green Bay Packers to six league titles, but the team never had played a championship game in Green Bay. When the playoff system was established in 1933, Lambeau moved the Packers' 1939 title game with the New York Giants from City Stadium in Green Bay to State Fair Park in Milwaukee because he thought he could and would get a bigger gate in the Wisconsin metropolis.

The people in Green Bay resented it. The team was the Green Bay Packers, mind you, not the Milwaukee Packers. They never forgot it, and 22 years later Vince Lombardi knew it, too, even though the Packers continued to play part of their home schedule in Milwaukee County Stadium. He met with the team's Executive Committee before the 1961 season began and said, "I've got news for you. If I win this thing this year, I want it in Green Bay."

"Welcome to Titletown USA." That's the message the Giants got upon arrival in Green Bay for their December 31, 1961, showdown with Lombardi's Packers. The signs were plastered everywhere—on storefronts, windows, billboards, hotel lobbies, car bumpers, telephone poles, jackets. Green Bay was ecstatic.

> *"Lombardi was tough and abusive and at times he was downright nasty."*
>
> **—BART STARR**

The Giants got an eyeful. On the bus ride from the airport to the team's headquarters at the Northland Hotel in downtown Green Bay, Sam Huff gazed from his seat and yelled to his teammates, "Look, they spelled Tittle wrong," referring to the Giants quarterback Y. A. Tittle. It was a typical loudmouth Huff line, brash and sarcastic. He was convinced New York was going to win the NFL championship in what they considered a small Midwest outpost. So were his teammates.

2

The Giants were a confident team. They had acquired Tittle from the San Francisco 49ers and wide receiver Del Shofner from the Los Angeles Rams in the summer of 1961, and the pair had combined to help make up for the loss of Frank Gifford, who was sitting out the season after suffering a severe concussion in 1960. They had hard-running backs Alex Webster, Phil King, and Joel Wells; solid receivers Joe Walton and Kyle Rote; and a tough offensive line made up of Rosey Brown, Jack Stroud, Ray Wietecha, and Darrell Dess.

The Giants' defense was anchored by Huff in the middle and Andy Robustelli at defensive end. With Robustelli were tackles Dick Modzelewski and Rosey Grier and Jim Katcavage at the other end. It was the first defensive line to earn the "Fearsome Foursome" nickname, and they had lived up to everything that was said about them.

When the Giants rolled over in their hotel beds to answer the phone that cold morning in Green Bay, they heard the desk clerk cheerfully say, "Howdy, Packer-Backer. It's 8:00." For all the history, all the championships, there had been nothing like this one in the emotional life of a Green Bay fan. If an election were held to choose the most beloved city in the NFL, Green Bay, said Packers fans, would win in a landslide.

There was no question of how Green Bay fans felt as they paraded around City Stadium before the 1961 NFL championship game between the Packers and the New York Giants. The Packers trounced the Giants, 37–0, for their first title under Vince Lombardi.

Lombardi, a born New Yorker, took full advantage of everything Green Bay had to offer. It was a David versus Goliath mentality, and he was talking like a native son.

"He built it up so the thing was you were defending the pride of Green Bay as much as you were the pride of the Packers," defensive end Willie Davis said about Lombardi's zeal as he approached the big game. "It was big ol' New York against lil' ol' Green Bay. And we all knew how much it meant to him personally.

"He felt he had earned the right to be a head coach long before that, so when it became a reality he wanted to leave no doubt. There was an

NFL Commissioner Pete Rozelle felt right at home in Green Bay on New Year's Eve as he greeted fans before the kickoff at City Stadium.

incredible driving force behind him, and it was so obvious before the Giant game. It was like he wanted the Giants wiped out."

The Packers, who had lost to the Philadelphia Eagles, 17–13, in the 1960 NFL championship game in Philadelphia, had swept to the Western Conference championship with an 11–3 record, easily running away from the runner-up Detroit Lions who finished 8–5–1. Lombardi kept a close watch on the tight Eastern Conference race, where the Eagles, the Cleveland Browns, and the Giants battled throughout the entire season.

The Eastern Conference champion was not decided until the final game of the season when New York fought to a 7–7 draw with the Browns. That tie gave the Giants a 10–3–1 record, to edge out the Eagles, at 10–4.

The stage was set. Lombardi had the championship game he most wanted to play, matching his Packers with the Giants, a New York team whose starting lineups were filled with his former pupils, a team coached by Allie Sherman, the man whose job Lombardi might have had.

The Packers had defeated the Giants twice during the season, both times 20–17. The first win was an exhibition game in Green Bay, the second a

NFL CHAMPIONSHIP GAME
December 31, 1961

The Green Bay Packers vs. the New York Giants
City Stadium (later renamed Lambeau Field), Green Bay, Wisconsin
Score: Green Bay 37, New York 0
Attendance: 39,029

SCORING SUMMARY:

New York	0	0	0	0	– 0
Green Bay	0	24	10	3	– 37

GB: Hornung 6-yard run (Hornung kick)
GB: Dowler 13-yard pass from Starr (Hornung kick)
GB: R. Kramer 14-yard pass from Starr (Hornung kick)
GB: Hornung 17-yard field goal
GB: Hornung 22-yard field goal
GB: R. Kramer 13-yard pass from Starr (Hornung kick)
GB: Hornung 19-yard field goal

league game in Milwaukee. In the game that counted, Jesse Whittenton, a defensive back with the Packers, gambled and won, coming up with the play that turned the game. Instead of tackling Giants' running back Alex Webster who broke in the open, he went for the ball and stole it. That critical turnover in the fourth quarter set up Jim Taylor's winning touchdown run.

It appeared obvious that these teams were evenly matched, and that would tend to make the Packers' job of beating the Giants a third time in a season more difficult. But as Lombardi said, "This is a special game."

Lombardi had carefully put together a championship team. There was Taylor, a powerful fullback who combined with Paul Hornung to give the Packers the best inside-outside combination in the league. There was Bart Starr, the cool brains behind the Packers' brawn. There was Ray Nitschke, the savage linebacker. There were so many others: Forrest Gregg, Willie Davis, Herb Adderley, Jim Ringo, Willie Wood, Henry Jordan—all of whom later would be inducted into the Pro Football Hall of Fame—and

Jerry Kramer, Fuzzy Thurston, Bob Skoronski, Norm Masters, Boyd Dowler, Max McGee, Ron Kramer, Dave Hanner, Bill Quinlan, Bill Forrester, Jesse Whittenton, John Symank, and Hank Gremminger.

This truly was a machine, created in the image of its coach—tough, unrelenting, and merciless. "You can play this game only one way," Lombardi was fond of saying, "and that's all out, all the time. Anything less is inexcusable."

But there was something that seriously threatened Lombardi's drive to his first championship. President Kennedy and the Department of Defense had activated thousands of military reservists and national guardsmen in response to the Berlin crisis. More than two dozen pro football players were called, but the Packers were hurt more than any other team. Three starters—Hornung, Nitschke, and Dowler—were among those summoned, and the coach was furious.

"They're doing a good job on us," Lombardi fumed. "You can't lose three frontliners and keep winning."

6

The Pentagon granted many players weekend passes to rejoin their teams. Dowler and Nitschke got leaves and played in every game with the Packers. But Hornung missed two, including the final game against the Rams. And now it looked like the Golden Boy, the league's most valuable player, would miss the championship game because his Christmas furlough would be up before the game.

Lombardi, though, had close connections with President Kennedy. He had endorsed Kennedy in a 1960 Wisconsin primary. A grateful future president never forgot. Neither did Lombardi.

He called the White House, and within an hour he was talking to the most powerful man in the world. The coach mentioned that Hornung had been called up and wouldn't be able to play against the Giants. The president instantly replied, "Paul Hornung isn't going to win the war on Sunday, but the football fans of this country deserve the two best teams on the field that day."

Hornung had been bothered all season with a chronic shoulder injury and pinched neck nerve, the result of playing this violent game. He thought the injuries would keep him from passing the army physical. "Anybody with that kind of injury who was called up for military service was 4-F," Hornung said.

Alex Webster, the Giants' workhorse running back, couldn't break this tackle as Willie Davis (No. 87) rushed in for support. The Packers held Webster to 19 yards in seven attempts.

Ron Kramer, the Big Oaf, leapt high to catch Bart Starr's pass; Giants' defenders Allan Webb (No. 21), Joe Morrison (No. 40), and Sam Huff (No. 70) could do little but watch.

The doctor at the induction center in Milwaukee first told him his condition could classify him as 4-F. But the doctor also told him that if he flunked Hornung, they would send him somewhere else until he passed. The Hornung case became a political football. On November 14, Mr. Touchdown was assigned to Fort Riley, Kansas, and became Private Hornung.

But Kennedy's call to Fort Riley changed things dramatically. Hornung will never forget it.

"Kennedy calls Fort Riley and asks to speak to the company commander, who was not there, so he finally gets the company captain," Hornung recalled. "And he says, 'This is President Kennedy and I'm calling on behalf of Paul Hornung,' and the company captain says, 'Yeah, and I'm Mickey Mouse.' He didn't believe it was him.

"Kennedy said he would like them to do him a favor and get my Christmas vacation leave changed. He asked that they get hold of my commanding officer and see if [they could] get this done. They got it changed. And I left."

On Christmas Eve Hornung arrived from Fort Riley and joined Nitschke and Dowler for a week of preparation for the big game. Now everything was in place. Only the Giants stood between Lombardi and the world championship.

All his life, or so it seemed, Vince Lombardi had prepared for this day. All the years of coaching at St. Cecilia High School in Englewood, New Jersey, being an assistant at Fordham and at West Point, and being an assistant with the Giants had come to this. All the planning, meetings, practices, drafting, trading—all the things that go into the makeup of an NFL champion had been pointing to this game. He was ready.

Lombardi was feeling his oats as Sunday drew near. On the night before the game Vince and his wife, Marie, invited a group of New York friends to dinner at the Stratosphere Club northeast of town on the road to Door County. The contingent was led by Wellington Mara, owner of the Giants and one of Lombardi's closest friends.

"There were four or five couples and a few priests and we had a great time," Mara recalled. "I remember thinking to myself how relaxed he was, how much he'd changed. I found out a moment after that how much I'd misjudged him. He stood up, signed the check he called for, and said, 'You can find your own way back to town.' Then he left. It was like he was saying that the game officially began then. It was a helluva long cab ride."

Before the game, Lombardi had expressed concern, not so much for the Giants as for the condition of the City Stadium field. It was buried under

9

"Lombardi had a hard exterior, but he also had a big, soft heart."

—RAY NITSCHKE

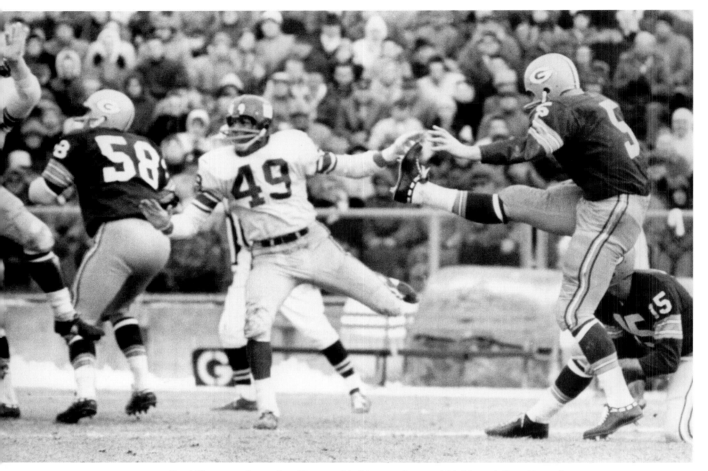

Paul Hornung beat the Giants with his running and kicking ability. Here, he connected on a 17-yard field goal, with Bart Starr holding and Dan Currie (No. 58) blocking; Erich Barnes of the Giants couldn't get close enough to block it. Hornung connected on all three of his field-goal attempts.

a heavy tarpaulin, a foot of hay, and 14 inches of snow. "If the field is in good condition, so are we," he said. "If the ground isn't frozen, our blockers will be able to get their footholds. Taylor and Hornung will be able to cut, and our receivers can make all the fakes and execute all the tricky moves to get clear.

"If all these things happen, we'll win."

Starting at 5:00 that Sunday morning, the ground crew began clearing the field at City Stadium. They shoveled off the layer of snow, then removed the covering of straw, and finally rolled back the canvas tarp that had protected the grass since the last home game in November. Lombardi found the field just as he had hoped: hard but not frozen.

The temperature was 21 degrees and the wind 10 miles per hour out of the west, balmy conditions for December 31 in Green Bay, as the stadium

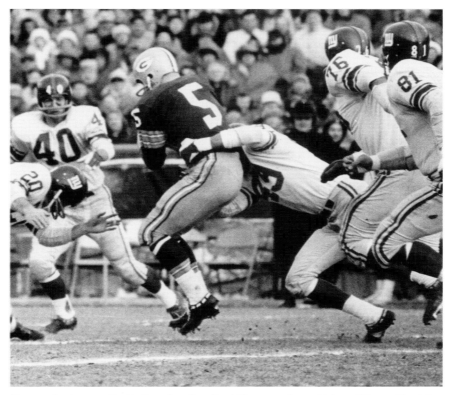

Five against one—that's the situation Paul Hornung found himself in as Giants' defenders Jim Patton (No. 20), Joe Morrison (No. 40), Cliff Livingston (making the tackle), Roosevelt Grier (No. 76), and Andy Robustelli (No. 81) chased the Golden Boy.

filled to 39,029, about 1,000 under capacity. Tickets, priced at $10, were selling on the street for $5 before the game.

City Stadium was rocking. The Packers' return to the championship game was the NFL's best story. The fans made it ear-splittingly clear that this was the greatest day ever. Heaven could wait. It would have to.

Nearly 40,000 people, bundled up against the cold, were watching as a single figure ran out of the north tunnel of the stadium. It was the sight of Paul Hornung. The crowd stood up and cheered as one. It was as though they were saying, "Have no fear, No. 5 is here."

"When Lombardi said, 'You were chosen to be a Packer,' he made it sound like something unique and wonderful."

—WILLIE DAVIS

There was a real difference between the two teams. The Giants thought they could win. The Packers, with the return of the Golden Boy, *knew* they could win.

It was a simple game plan that Lombardi had designed, one that could have been designed by Attila. Keep the swords swinging until there were no more heads to roll. Give no quarter. Take no prisoners.

12

The Giants won the toss and elected to receive as the temperature nudged over 20. Lombardi had arranged for Ben Agajanian to back up Paul Hornung as a kicker. "Vince wanted to use me on kickoffs because he didn't want Paul to get hurt," Agajanian recalled. "I said, 'Thanks a lot.' I'm 42 and Paul is a young kid." Agajanian booted a short kick that Wells returned to the Giants' 30-yard line. At first, the Giants and Packers went after each other like two heavyweight boxers, testing each other with short jabs.

However, one play early in the first quarter set the tone of the game for the Giants. Kyle Rote got open in the Green Bay secondary and dropped Tittle's pass. He had probably caught 100 passes like that during his career, but this one was critical. Then he dropped another, and it became obvious the Giants weren't ready to play on the frozen tundra.

The Giants' opening series ended with a punt. Their second possession ended with a punt, and the Packers drove 80 yards and scored when Hornung wheeled in from the 6-yard line and then kicked the extra point. Their third series ended with an interception when Tittle's pass was tipped by Henry Jordan and picked off by Nitschke. In six plays the Packers scored their second touchdown as Starr fired a 13-yard pass to Dowler and Hornung converted. The Giants' fourth drive ended when Hank

SEASON RECORD

DATE	OPPONENT	W/L	GB	OPP	LOC	ATTENDANCE
9/17/61	Detroit Lions	L	13	17	Milw	44,307
9/24/61	San Francisco 49ers	W	30	10	GB	38,669
10/01/61	Chicago Bears	W	24	0	GB	38,669
10/08/61	Baltimore Colts	W	45	7	GB	38,669
10/15/61	Cleveland Browns	W	49	17	Cle	75,049
10/22/61	Minnesota Vikings	W	33	7	Minn	42,007
10/29/61	Minnesota Vikings	W	28	10	Milw	44,116
11/05/61	Baltimore Colts	L	21	45	Balt	57,641
11/12/61	Chicago Bears	W	31	28	Chi	49,711
11/19/61	Los Angeles Rams	W	35	17	GB	38,669
11/23/61	Detroit Lions	W	17	9	Det	55,662
12/03/61	New York Giants	W	20	17	Milw	47,012
12/10/61	San Francisco 49ers	L	21	22	SF	55,722
12/17/61	Los Angeles Rams	W	24	17	LA	49,169

NFL CHAMPIONSHIP

DATE	OPPONENT	W/L	GB	OPP	LOC	ATTENDANCE
12/31/61	New York Giants	W	37	0	GB	39,029

Gremminger intercepted Tittle's pass at midfield and returned to the New York 36. In eight plays Green Bay stretched its lead to 21–0 when Starr passed 14 yards to Ron Kramer and Hornung added the extra point.

The Giants' only threat came when old Chuck Conerly, wearing sneakers, replaced Tittle at quarterback midway through the second quarter. Conerly moved the Giants from their 39-yard line to the Green Bay 6-yard line, but the drive ended on a fourth down incomplete pass.

You could see New York's battery run down when the Packers stormed back and Hornung kicked a 17-yard field goal to give Green Bay a 24–0 halftime lead. This was Miss versus Match. Sherman made no changes at halftime.

"We didn't even go to the blackboard," the Giants coach said. "You can't do anything on a blackboard about dropped passes and fumbles. These were the things that were hurting us."

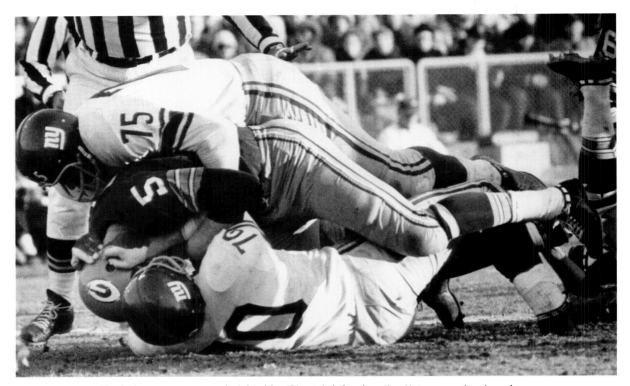

Paul Hornung was sandwiched by Giants' defenders Jim Katcavage (top) and Sam Huff.

The point is, the Giants were simply outclassed. The Packers' dominance was beyond dispute.

It was like being run over by a truck. A Mack truck. There were Packer tire tracks all over City Stadium.

If the Giants were going to move the ball they would have to prove their air attack was willing and, most of all, able.

"When we got behind like that, the Green Bay defensive line dared us to run," said Giants tackle Greg Larson. "They knew we had to pass to catch up. They came in swinging from the heels, with fists and forearms and elbows. It was the most awesome thing I've ever been involved in. We had no way to stop them. They were like wild men. It was unending, it seemed. They constantly punished us."

The Packers came out of the dressing room in combat boots as the second half started. They continued to pound the Giants. Hornung kicked his second field goal, Ron Kramer caught his second touchdown pass, and Hornung added another field goal. That's how they played this game—all of them.

Paul Hornung, escorted by teammate Ron Kramer (No. 88), drew a crowd of gang-tackling Giants, including Jim Patton (No. 20) and Cliff Livingston (No. 89), as they tried to stop the Packers' great halfback.

Willie Wood leapt high to break up Y. A. Tittle's pass intended for Joe Walton while Packer teammate Hank Gremminger closed in.

You want heroes? Throw the whole deck of cards up in the air and pick them up in any order.

There was Hornung, who ran for 89 yards and scored 19 points—6 with his feet and 13 with his toe—a new individual championship scoring mark. He played with only five days of practice.

There was Bart Starr, who methodically picked the Giants defense to pieces, completing 10 of 17 passes for 164 yards and three touchdowns and no interceptions.

There was Ron Kramer—the Big Oaf—who blasted the way for Hornung and Taylor to run to daylight and bullied his way into the end zone for touchdowns passes of 14 and 13 yards, dragging Giants defenders with him.

Bart Starr's pass, intended for Boyd Dowler, was deflected before the Packers' big flanker could catch it while defender Erich Barnes (No. 49) closed in and Sam Huff (No. 70) watched. Dowler, on leave from the army, caught three passes for 37 yards, including a touchdown.

The Packers intercepted four Giants' passes, and Herb Adderley's pick on the second from the last play of the game punctuated the shutout by the Packers' defense. Tittle gave hopeless chase to Adderley while Del Shofner (No. 85) was already out of the play.

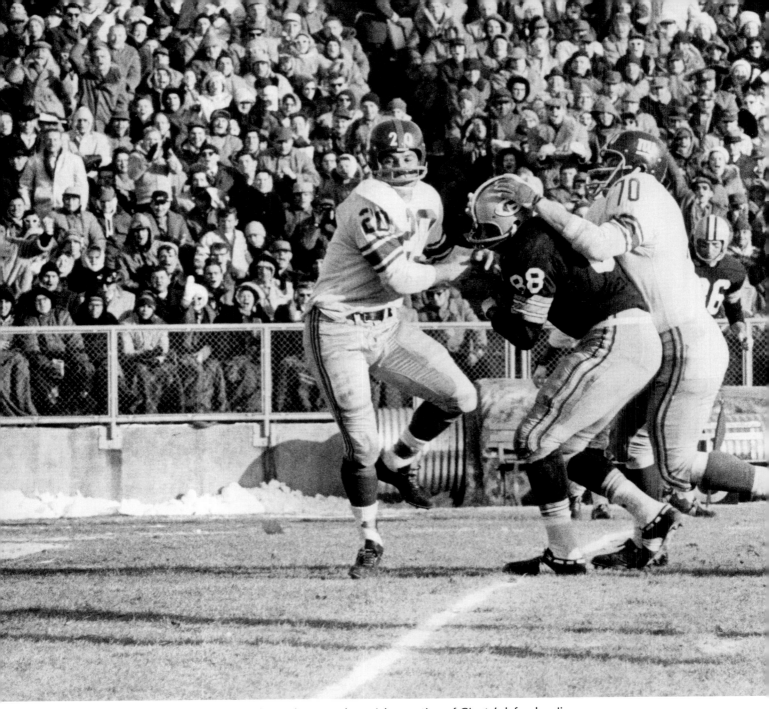

Ron Kramer of the Packers got the quick attention of Giants' defenders Jimmy Patton and Sam Huff, but they couldn't stop the burly tight end from scoring a touchdown. Kramer caught four passes for 80 yards, including two for touchdowns.

There was Nitschke, who led a defense that picked off four New York passes, made jarring tackles, and kept a battered Tittle worrying where he was lining up.

What the onslaught produced was a Green Bay offense that controlled the ball forever. The Packers ran off 63 plays to the Giants' 43. They rushed for 181 yards to New York's 31. They passed for 164 yards to the Giants' 119.

"The harder you work, the harder it is to surrender."

—VINCE LOMBARDI

The Packers picked up 19 first downs to New York's 6. The Packers took the ball away on four interceptions and a fumble recovery and did not turn the ball over to the Giants.

21

As the game turned into a complete rout, New York coach Allie Sherman tried to encourage Joe Walton, Kyle Rote, and Alex Webster on the Giants' sideline during a timeout.

As the game raced out of control for the Giants, Jim Taylor and coach Vince Lombardi remained stiff-lipped on the Packers' sideline while Green Bay continued to pile it on New York.

The Packers had played an almost perfect game. In the winners' locker room, Lombardi said, "Today, this was the greatest team in the history of the National Football League. Defensively, we were outstanding, and our offense was superb.

"It was a tremendous team effort all around, by both units, so I don't care to single out different players. But today Paul Hornung was a great,

great player. We couldn't use Jimmy Taylor [nursing an injured back] too much, but Paul picked us up and did a terrific job."

Hornung, a Jeep driver at Fort Riley, was selected the game's outstanding player and given a Corvette. Explaining his extraordinary game, he laughed and said, "I'm just a fantastic athlete." Then he got more serious and added, "I was just ready to play. That was our best football team. I wanted us to score 70 points on them, but Vince didn't. We could have scored 70 points that day."

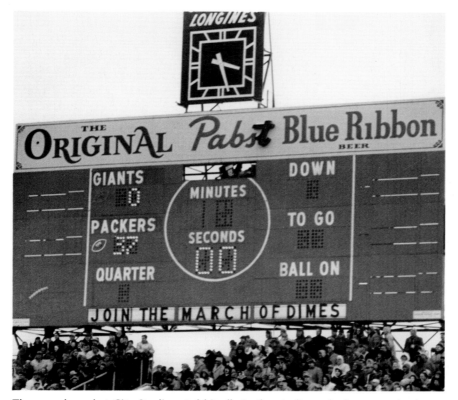

The scoreboard at City Stadium told it all. As the stadium clock approached 3:30, the Packers were the new kings of the NFL.

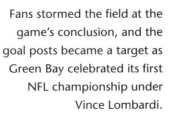
24

Fans stormed the field at the
game's conclusion, and the
goal posts became a target as
Green Bay celebrated its first
NFL championship under
Vince Lombardi.

Lombardi started taking his starters out of the game in the fourth quarter. It was out of respect for the Maras. He didn't want to rub it in.

The Giants were left exhausted—like skiers on a chairlift at the end of a long day. The Packers had delivered their closing arguments as the NFL's best team, right between New York's eyes.

Paul Hornung's smile spoke volumes as Vince Lombardi was carried off the field by Dan Currie (not shown) and Dave Hanner after the Packers' shocking demolition of the Giants.

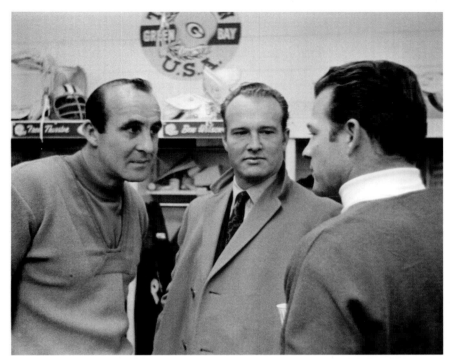

Frank Gifford (right) visits Max McGee (left) and Paul Hornung in the winners' locker room after the Packers had humiliated the Giants. The former Giants' star halfback retired after the 1960 season and worked for CBS television. Gifford returned to the Giants in 1962 as a flanker back.

The players lifted Lombardi on their shoulders. Fans swarmed the field and jumped on the south goal post until it fell to the ground. The Packers' band played "Auld Lang Syne" as New Year's Eve approached. And the crowd headed for the bars.

"Set 'em up, bartender, and pour 'em like you don't own it," they yelled. "Tonight we toast the Green Bay Packers, best football team in the world."

Little did they know that it would get a lot better.

"You might reduce Lombardi's coaching philosophy to a single sentence: in any game, you do the things you do best and you do them over and over and over."

—GEORGE HALAS

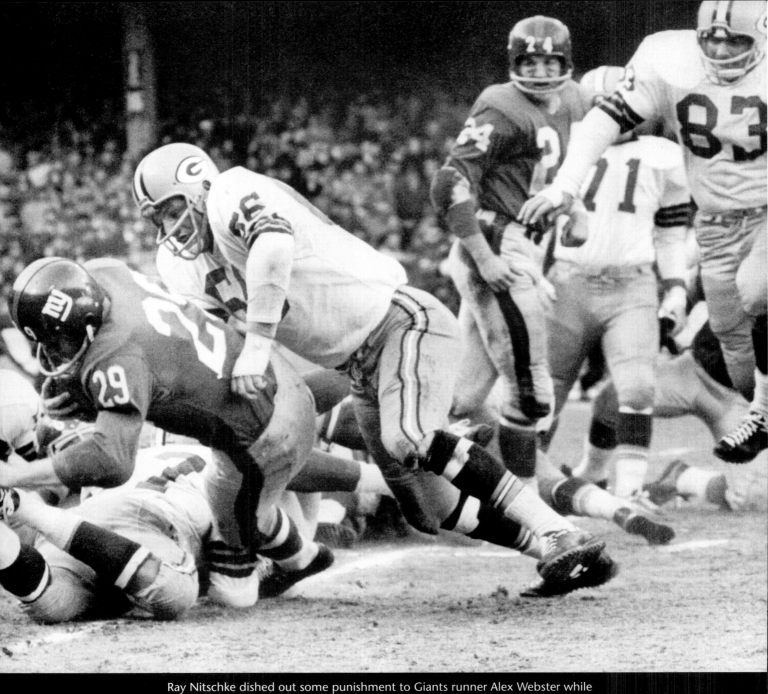

Ray Nitschke dished out some punishment to Giants runner Alex Webster while
Bill Quinlan (No. 83) came in hippity-hoppity a bit too late. Webster led the
Giants' running attack with 19 yards in seven carries. Nitschke was named the
game's most valuable player.

CHAPTER 2

THE 1962 NFL CHAMPIONSHIP GAME

To understand what the 1962 National Football League championship was all about, you start with the stadium. Yankee Stadium, the house that Ruth built, was rich in tradition, home to one of the greatest dynasties in sports—the New York Yankees—and to many big-time sports attractions.

It also was home to the New York football Giants, starting in 1956. For all of its historical charms, it was a poor place for football with its bad sight lines for fans, cramped locker rooms for players, and miserable working conditions for the press as the weather got colder.

Vince Lombardi loved the place. He loved New York. He loved the Yankees. He loved legends. Back in Green Bay, he had installed a sign above the locker room door before the team headed for New York and the 1962 NFL championship game: "Home of the Green Bay Packers, the Yankees of Football." He was confident his Packers would become legends.

Yankee Stadium is where he had worked for five years as offensive coordinator of the Giants. And on this late December afternoon this Brooklyn-born coach was the enemy bringing his powerful Packers into Yankee Stadium for a rematch title game with the Giants. The Giants, a team whose uniforms came equipped with shoulder chips, were so fired up for this game that they would have played the Packers any time, any place—for a keg of beer.

"Some of us will do our jobs well and some will not, but we will all be judged by only one thing—the result."

—VINCE LOMBARDI

The Packers had practiced in Green Bay until Friday and then flew to New York and set up quarters at the Hotel Manhattan. The New York newspapers were on strike and not publishing. That was just fine with Lombardi, who figured he wouldn't have to deal with the press until Sunday.

That all changed with one call Saturday afternoon. Vince and Marie were sitting in their hotel suite, chatting with friends, when the phone rang. Vince picked it up.

"No, no. I'm too busy," he said. "I tell you it's out of the question. Forget it."

It was Jim Kenzil, the league's chief publicist. Kenzil informed him that a big press conference had been set up at another hotel. It was about to start, but everyone was waiting for the emperor of Green Bay to arrive.

Lombardi started arguing with Kenzil. He said no one had told him about the press conference and that he could not attend because he promised his parents that he and his family would go and see them in New Jersey.

The phone rang again. This time it was Pete Rozelle, the commissioner, and for once Lombardi lost an argument.

Reluctantly, Lombardi put on his coat and hat and took a cab to the Americana. He walked briskly into the press room without removing his hat and coat. Kenzil informed the gathering of mostly New York writers that Lombardi would be available for only a few questions because of a prior commitment.

There were a few lightweight questions to loosen up the coach. Then Dick Young, syndicated columnist for the *New York Daily News*, spoke.

"Vinnie, you are coming back to your hometown for a championship game. Do you think there's any chance the officials might tend to be homers?" Young asked.

Lombardi snorted. His face grew red. He glared at Young as if Young was some pip-squeak reporter from Sheboygan.

Although they were strictly in the minority in New York, Green Bay fans made their appearance felt in the Big Apple. Here, they showed their support in front of the Packers' hotel.

"That's the silliest question I've ever heard," he said, raising his voice in anger. Then he turned on his heel and walked out of the room. The press conference was over.

The Packers were a dominant football team in 1962. They repeated as Western Conference champions, finishing 13–1. They outscored their collective opponents by an almost three-to-one margin, 415 points to 148.

Their only loss came on Thanksgiving Day at Detroit when the Lions humiliated the Packers, 26–14. The Packers trailed, 26–0, going into the

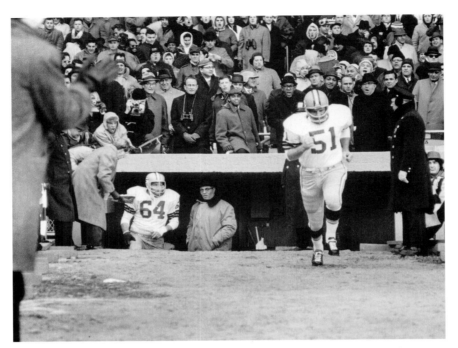

The New York fans laughed and jeered in Yankee Stadium when the Packers came out of the visitors' dugout to be introduced. Center Jim Ringo (No. 51) was the first to come out, followed by guard Jerry Kramer, while coach Vince Lombardi waited impatiently.

fourth quarter. The whole country sat back and watched on television as Roger Brown and Joe Schmidt and Alex Karras took turns smothering Bart Starr. They sacked him 11 times. The Lions netted 300 yards in the game; the Packers 132.

The media covering the game at Tiger Stadium didn't know what to expect when, after a cooling-off period, they were allowed into the Packers' locker room. They expected the worst from Lombardi. They were amazed at what they saw.

Lombardi was laughing. Turning to his critics, he said, "You didn't think we were going to win them all, did you?"

This was not the time to show anger. It was time to use some psychology and ease up. He knew he could get the whip out next week. He knew

New York fans saved their loudest boos for Jim Taylor. Coach Vince Lombardi had big plans for his tough-as-nails fullback.

The weather was so brutal that Vince Lombardi had to shed his customary camel hair coat and wear a heavy team overcoat as he returned to Yankee Stadium with the Packers. Lombardi said he had never seen a worse day for football.

he would have a very coachable team when it went back to work in preparation for the next game.

"He was very realistic after the game," defensive end Willie Davis said. "He didn't blow up. He didn't seem upset. He just said the right things. He said, 'The real glory is being knocked to your knees and then coming back.'"

Lombardi said everyone had been too confident—the players, the press, but mostly himself. In the week before the Detroit game, he had allowed a television crew inside team meetings for a report on the making of an undefeated season. No more of that.

The Packers stormed back like champions. They hammered the Los Angeles Rams, 41–10, in Milwaukee and then headed to the West Coast where they beat the San Francisco 49ers, 31–21, and the Rams again in the LA Coliseum, 20–17.

Lombardi had a juggernaut. This was a veteran team with talent everyplace. Jim Taylor earned the NFL rushing title with 1,474 yards and scored 19 touchdowns. Bart Starr was the league's passing champion, and Willie Wood was the leader in interceptions.

The Giants? Well, the Giants had spent the entire year waiting for this day. They said they never wanted a game more than this one. They wanted to show their fans and the world that what happened to them a year ago in Green Bay had been a 37–0 fluke.

For the two weeks before the championship game, there was a sign hanging prominently in the Giants' locker room. It had no words, just a number: 37. The numerals were two feet high.

The Giants were playing angry. They were on a mission. They had beat up on opponents all season and finished 12–2. Their date with destiny had come.

"That game was the low point of my career," defensive end Andy Robustelli said, recalling the 1961 debacle at Green Bay. "We have done a great deal with defense for the Giants, and that one really stings. It burned into my brain, and the only way I can get rid of the memory is by returning the aggravation. If we win this game it won't be enough. We have to destroy the Packers and Lombardi. It's the only way we can atone for what happened to us last year."

Despite the one-sidedness of the 1961 game, many observers felt the Giants would have the edge. They were seething for revenge, and they were playing at home. There would be no excuses. None.

And the weather, New Yorkers believed, could not be as bad as it had been in Green Bay the year before. It wasn't. It was worse.

How bad was it? It was atrocious. The temperature dipped from 20 at game time to 17 at the half to 10 at the end. What made it unbearable was the incessant wind. Forty-mile-per-hour gusts exploded across the frozen stadium, whipping an acre of dirt and

35

"There wasn't any jealousy on the club, no envy of, say, one particular receiver making All-Pro and the other not making it. We had as much unity as you possibly could have, which goes along with the love aspect Lombardi always talked about."

—JIM TAYLOR

debris into a swirling storm. Newspapers and trash blew across the field. The teams' benches were blown over. Occasionally a fan's hat would blow on the field. Once, the hat belonged to Lombardi.

It was a day polar bears and penguins would seek shelter. Those who played in it remember it as the coldest game they had ever played—colder than even the Ice Bowl game five years later in sub-zero Green Bay.

When the teams came out for warm-ups, it was clear the elements would play a key role in this championship game. The grassless field was like concrete. It was hard, frozen in large swatches, with holes and ruts everywhere.

The stiff winds blew straight across the field. Yet, from time to time the two large flags on the poles in centerfield whipped straight out in opposite directions. That was how tricky the wind was.

For the 64,892 frozen fans sitting in this concrete igloo, the howling wind was all they thought it would be and worse. Players couldn't catch passes or field punts because the ball danced without reason or pattern through the gusts.

When Bart Starr and Y. A. Tittle tried to throw, the ball would start blowing back to them. The wind played such havoc that a New York assistant turned to coach Allie Sherman and said, "We just lost our passing game."

Lombardi called it the worst playing conditions imaginable. But in his heart he knew the wind took the teeth out of Tittle's long bombs.

Yankee Stadium had all the charm of a municipal warehouse as Willie Wood kicked off for the Packers. Wood placed the ball on a tee, but it blew off twice. Finally, he called a teammate over to hold the ball, and the game began.

What followed was one of the most violent of all NFL championship games. A game that was billed as the grudge rematch for the 1961 title game ended in a quest for survival. If they had fought this one in a bar, the cops would have stopped it. They would have arrested Sam Huff, No. 70, middle linebacker with the Giants.

"We went right after Sam Huff because Sam Huff was supposed to be the best linebacker around and going after him and defeating him underscored the weak points in their defense."

—JIM RINGO

In the gusty, fitful winds at Yankee Stadium, guard/kicker Jerry Kramer nailed a 26-yard field goal in the first quarter to put the Packers on the scoreboard first. Green Bay's only touchdown came on a seven-yard run by Jim Taylor. The rest of the game's scoring belonged to Kramer, the straight-ahead kicker, who connected on two more field goals—from 29 and 30 yards away.

1962 NFL CHAMPIONSHIP
December 30, 1962

The Green Bay Packers vs. the New York Giants
Yankee Stadium, the Bronx, New York
Score: Green Bay 16, New York 7
Attendance: 64,892

SCORING SUMMARY:

Green Bay	3	7	3	3 -	16
New York	0	0	7	0 -	7

GB: J. Kramer 26-yard field goal
GB: Taylor 7-yard run (J. Kramer kick)
NY: Collier blocked punt recovery in end zone (Chandler kick)
GB: J. Kramer 29-yard field goal
GB: J. Kramer 30-yard field goal

There are those who said Huff was no more than a TV creation from a Madison Avenue imagination—the Violent World of Sam Huff. They called him a glory-seeker, a pile-on tackler, a cheap-shot artist.

Huff was more or less the patsy of the Packers' 37–0 rout in 1961. The Packers ran at him and over him, and when the game was over his reputation lay in shreds.

This time Huff was ready. The Giants, led by Huff, came slashing after the Packers. They were likened to escapees from a correctional institution.

To them, it was the bigger the star, the bigger the target. No star was bigger than Jim Taylor, the Packers' sledgehammer of a fullback. Taylor was built like a cast-iron statue. When he saw a clear field ahead he would hunt down a defender to run into. After a 1960 game with the Bears, Lombardi made his fullback watch game film of going out of his way to run over the Chicago safety.

"What are you trying to do out there?" Lombardi asked. "You gotta sting 'em a little bit, Coach," Taylor replied. "You know you've gotta make those tacklers respect you."

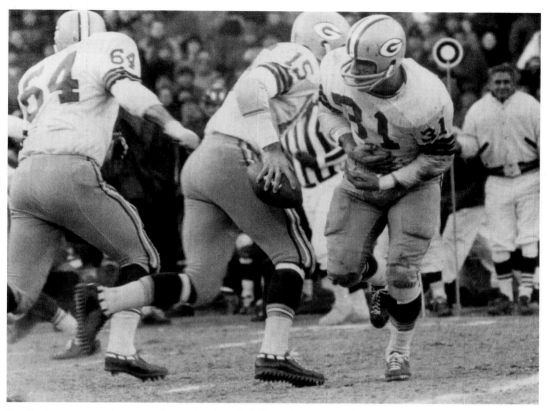

Jim Taylor was on his way as he took a handoff from Bart Starr. The Packers' fullback carried the ball a career-high 31 times, gained 85 yards, and scored the team's only touchdown.

"They respect him," Lombardi wrote in his book *Run to Daylight*. "In fact every time he carries the ball there are 11 of them, all of whom want to pay their respects to him personally."

Early in the game, Taylor took a handoff from Starr and headed directly for Huff, but he couldn't cut on the icy surface. As Huff drove Taylor out of bounds, he used his knees and elbows to full advantage as the two men skidded across the ice.

Taylor struggled to his feet and leaned over, coughing blood. He wobbled back to the Packers huddle and told Starr to give him the ball again.

Rosey Grier, the Giants' 6'5", 290-pound defensive tackle, broke through the block of Fuzzy Thurston (No. 63) to nail Green Bay quarterback Bart Starr for a loss.

Taylor carried the ball 31 times, gained 85 yards, and scored the Packers' only touchdown. He had to fight for every yard. The Giants threw everything at him.

"We couldn't throw the ball because of the swirling wind," Taylor said. "We just tried to come off the ball and run to daylight. They ran me out of bounds so much because I couldn't cut up field. I ended up with 31 carries. A career high. I had 27, 28, but never up to 30."

Taylor looked gaunt. He had lost 10 pounds.

"It was the suffering together that made the Packers a great team. And Vince made them suffer."

—TOM LANDRY

It would not be known until weeks later than he had hepatitis. He bit his tongue and was spitting blood throughout the game, and his gashed elbow had to be stitched up at halftime.

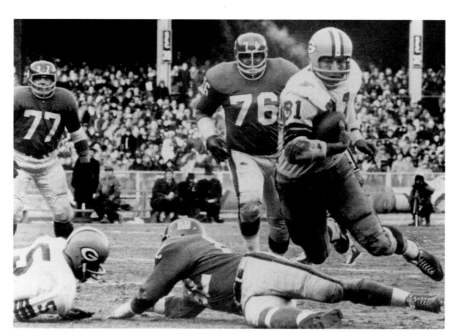

This was the only play on which the Giants didn't touch Jim Taylor. Scoring the game's only touchdown from the 7-yard line, Taylor ran over a fallen defender en route to the New York end zone while all Dick Modzelewski (No. 77) and Rosey Grier (No. 76) could do was watch.

Del Shofner, a big weapon in the Giants' offense, looked for daylight after catching a Y. A. Tittle pass. Shofner caught five passes for 69 yards—none of them for big yardage.

For the Giants, it was "I-got-him, you-got-him" football. Beat the stuffing out of him. Almost every time Taylor was tackled it ended up with three or four Giants piling on and Huff, the ringleader, giving Taylor an extra shot into the frozen turf, or knee into the groin, and telling Taylor that he stunk.

"Did everything I could to that sonofabitch," Huff said later. After Taylor cut back and scored on a seven-yard touchdown run, he turned to his tormentor in the Giants' end zone and said, "How do I smell from here, Sam?"

It was an elemental struggle. Taylor was on the ropes getting hammered with no referee to stop the fight. He deserved the Bronze Star. It was a feat of epic toughness. It's one thing to play in pain. It's quite another to play well.

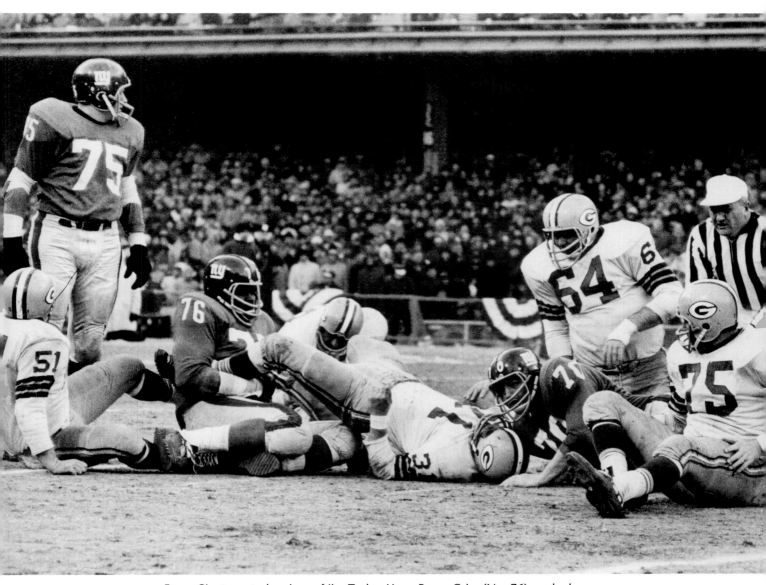

Every Giant wanted a piece of Jim Taylor. Here, Rosey Grier (No. 76) worked on Taylor's leg; Sam Huff was down after hitting the Packer fullback high. Linemen Jim Ringo (No. 51), Jerry Kramer (No. 64), and Forrest Gregg (No. 75) watched as Taylor retained a firm grip on the football.

Jim Taylor doubled up in pain as he headed back to the Packers' bench.

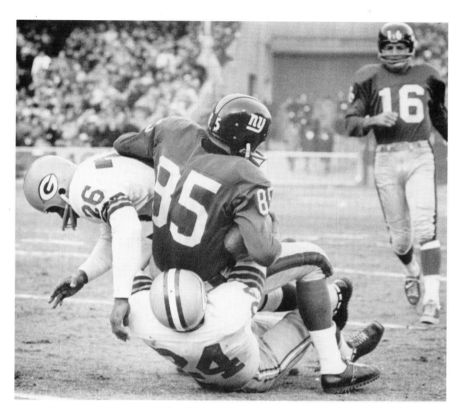

Willie Wood and Herb Adderley (No. 26) made sure Del Shofner stayed put after catching a Y. A. Tittle pass; Frank Gifford (No. 16) arrived late for support.

Some people will tell you that pro football isn't such a complicated game. You line up. He hits you in the mouth; you hit him in the mouth. The tougher guy wins. It's the people, the athletes, who make the difference.

After the game, Huff said: "Taylor isn't human. No human being could have taken the punishment he got today. Every time he was tackled it was like crashing him down on a concrete sidewalk because the ground was as hard as pavement. But he kept bouncing up, snarling at us and asking for more."

In the end, the job of determining the outcome of the game was left to Jerry Kramer, the Packers' left guard. Paul Hornung, because of a knee

Jim Taylor broke clear with New York defenders Dick Lynch (left) and Sam Huff in hot pursuit. After the game, Huff said, "Taylor isn't human. No human could have taken the punishment he got today."

injury, was no longer the team's place-kicker. Kramer was. It was the first time in the offensive lineman's career that his toe made the difference on the scoreboard.

Kramer was pumped up for the game. He had not been able to play in the 1961 championship game because of a broken leg.

"In the beginning when I lined up for that first field goal, I'm thinking to myself, 'I'm kicking a field goal in Yankee Stadium and across the line are Huff and Robustelli and Modzelewski and all the great New York

SEASON RECORD

DATE	OPPONENT	W/L	GB	OPP	LOC	ATTENDANCE
9/16/62	Minnesota Vikings	W	34	7	GB	38,669
9/23/62	St. Louis Cardinals	W	17	0	Milw	44,885
9/30/62	Chicago Bears	W	49	0	GB	38,669
10/7/62	Detroit Lions	W	9	7	GB	38,669
10/14/62	Minnesota Vikings	W	48	21	Minn	41,475
10/21/62	San Francisco 49ers	W	31	13	Milw	46,010
10/28/62	Baltimore Colts	W	17	6	Balt	57,966
11/4/62	Chicago Bears	W	38	7	Chi	48,753
11/11/62	Philadelphia Eagles	W	49	0	Phil	60,671
11/18/62	Baltimore Colts	W	17	13	GB	38,669
11/22/62	Detroit Lions	L	14	26	Det	57,578
12/2/62	Los Angeles Rams	W	41	10	Milw	46,833
12/09/62	San Francisco 49ers	W	31	21	SF	53,769
12/16/62	Los Angeles Rams	W	20	17	LA	60,389

NFL CHAMPIONSHIP

DATE	OPPONENT	W/L	GB	OPP	LOC	ATTENDANCE
12/30/62	New York Giants	W	16	7	NY	64,892

Giants, and what the hell am I doing out here?' I just felt that I was totally out of place," Kramer said.

The All-Pro lineman thunked a 26-yard field goal into the swirling wind in the first quarter to give the Packers a 3–0 lead. When Taylor powered seven yards through the Giants in the second period, the Packers left the field with a 10–0 halftime lead.

The Giants got a big break in the second half. Max McGee, told to take over punting duties for the injured Boyd Dowler, never had a punt blocked in his life. Standing in the Green Bay end zone, McGee never had a chance as Erich Barnes, a fast defensive back, broke through and blocked the punt and Jim Collier, a substitute end, fell on it for a New York touchdown.

It was the Giants' only score and trimmed the Packer lead to 10–7. As the temperature moved down to 10 degrees and both teams had trouble moving the ball, the rest of the game's scoring belonged to Kramer, the straight-ahead kicker.

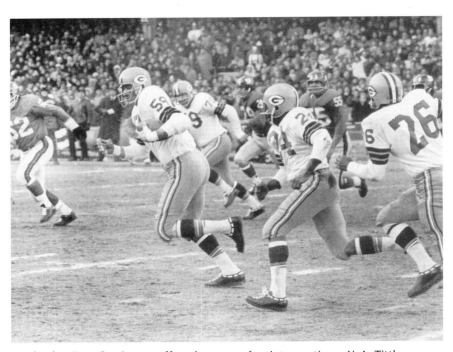

Linebacker Dan Currie was off to the races after intercepting a Y. A. Tittle pass that was deflected by Ray Nitschke. With an open route to the Giants' end zone and a convoy of blockers, Currie fell down on the Green Bay 40 with no enemy within shouting distance of him. His left knee, which had been severely damaged two months earlier in a game at Philadelphia, simply gave out.

Kramer always explained that his kicking job was like a golfer lining up a putt. He said, under normal conditions, he would try to pick up something in the background—a post, a brightly colored coat, a press box window. He would draw a line, keep his head down, and follow through.

But in these horrendous playing conditions, all Kramer could do was aim and pray. His second attempt, from the 37-yard line, in the first quarter was short and wide. Then he stepped up and booted a 29-yarder in the third period, missed one from the 40 in the fourth quarter, and thunked his final field goal home from the 30.

"I was a little nervous about kicking in Yankee Stadium," Kramer said later. "The first one, when I looked up, it looked like the ball was outside the goal posts, yet the official had his hands in the air signaling 'good' and

I said to Bart Starr [the holder], 'What the hell's he doing?' And Bart said, 'Shut up and get off the field.'"

Three out of five field-goal attempts was unbelievable under the circumstances. Kramer scored 10 points, including the placement after Taylor's touchdown. And he had helped open up the holes up front for Taylor. It was quite a game for an athlete with such an incredible medical history. He had endured 22 operations, most of them major, many of them the direct result of football injuries. He was given up for dead once; everyone including his doctors thought he had cancer. Lodged in his large

Protesting an interference penalty, Willie Wood (No. 24) inadvertently charged into back judge Thomas Kelleher, knocking him to the ground. Kelleher evicted Wood from the game and marched off a 15-yard penalty, moving the ball to the Green Bay 18. The Packers' defense then stopped the Giants cold.

Sam Huff (No. 70) led the Giants' charge all day against Taylor. "Did everything I could to that sonofabitch," the linebacker said later.

intestine were wooden splinters, the result of stepping on a loose plank while chasing a cow as a 17-year-old. Twelve years later they were removed and are now on display at the Packer Hall of Fame. He also suffered a chipped vertebra near his neck, a detached retina, and a broken ankle.

"Probably the biggest moment in my career was the final field goal when we sealed the victory," Kramer said. "All the guys were jumping on me. For an offensive guard, that doesn't happen."

Meanwhile, Ray Nitschke had the kind of game a middle linebacker can only dream of. Every time the Giants offense took the field it saw the whites of Nitschke's eyes. He recovered two fumbles and deflected a Tittle pass that was picked off by Dan Currie, the Packers' left linebacker. He might have added an interception of his own were it not for his hands being half frozen.

The Giants made one last serious threat. Aided by penalties, New York moved from its 20 to the Green Bay 47. Then Tittle passed to Del Shofner over the middle. The ball was wide of the mark, but Willie Wood, the Packers' safety, was charged with interference, moving the ball to the Green Bay 33.

When Wood got up to protest the call, he inadvertently charged into the official, back judge Thomas Kelleher, and knocked him to the ground. Kelleher got up, ejected Wood from the game, and marched off 15 more yards to the Green Bay 18.

A touchdown and extra point would have put the Giants ahead, 14–13. But the Packers' world-class defense took charge again and stopped the drive cold. The Giants' offense had not, in two championship games, scored on the Green Bay defense.

"You look back and you know that you had nothing left—nothing—and yet you still continued to play. Like that Giants game. No one knows until they are faced with it just how much pain they can endure, how much suffering, how much effort they have left. That's the way it was that day."

—JIM TAYLOR

51

Nitschke, for his heroics, was named the game's most valuable player and was awarded a sports car. Kramer got the game ball.

"This was probably our strongest team overall," Kramer said. "Jim and Paul were still strong and young, and Bart had come of age. And I think we all were cohesive, all strong, all full of it, and all hungry."

After the Packers got on the buses to take them to the airport, a Yankee Stadium maintenance man watched as the last player and equipment was put on the bus. Then, in a gruff voice, he said to the lead bus driver: "They're all in and ready to leave," he said. "Get those goddamn Packers out of New York!"

The champagne was flowing and the good times were rolling on the turbulent plane ride back to Green Bay for all but one person. Jim Taylor huddled alone in the back of the plane with an overcoat covering him. He was shaking and shivering.

"He got the absolute crap kicked out of him," Kramer said. "He was really hurting. But what a game he had."

Two weeks later, while preparing for the Pro Bowl game in Los Angeles, Taylor was diagnosed with hepatitis. He would recover and come back for more championship runs with the Packers.

Yankee Stadium would never again host an NFL championship game. The Giants would have better luck moving to Giants Stadium in New Jersey in 1976.

Boyd Dowler caught another pass before Cleveland defensive back Bernie
Parrish (No. 30) could tackle him. This was one of five receptions the Packers'
big flanker made, for a total of 59 yards.

CHAPTER 3

THE 1965

NFL CHAMPIONSHIP GAME

The man's name is Don Chandler. He was one of the first true specialists in the National Football League. He was a place-kicker and a punter, and he rarely got his uniform dirty.

He was the only player to carry three shoes into each game. There were one for his left foot and two for his right foot—an old-fashioned high-top with a squared-off toe for kicking field goals and a low-cut shoe for punting.

"Sometimes I feel like a one-armed paperhanger," Chandler would say, referring to the fact that he would change his footwear up to 10 times a game depending on whether the coach decided to go for a field goal or a punt. When the coach changed his mind, Chandler had to change his shoe. The low one wasn't bad, but lacing up the high-top took time.

Had it not been for Chandler and his gifted right foot, there would probably never have been a 1965 NFL title game in Green Bay—and what eventually led to an unprecedented three-straight league championships by the Packers. Chandler was the lifesaver.

The Packers had plenty of help getting Lambeau Field ready for the championship game after a five-inch snowstorm hit the area in the morning. Local citizens were more than happy to pitch in, clearing the snow from the stands and field.

It's not true that Vince Lombardi found Don Chandler by paging through the yellow pages. It's just that if you knew Lombardi, he could always find a player when he needed one—a backup quarterback in Zeke Bratkowski, a wide receiver in Carroll Dale, a linebacker in Lee Roy Caffey.

It was the lack of a kicker that hurt the Packers more than anything else in Green Bay's unsuccessful try for a title in 1964. The Packers went down to defeat three times in their first seven games by margins of two extra points and a field goal, and they finished 8–5–1.

Guard Jerry Kramer, the place-kicking hero of the 1962 championship game, had undergone no fewer than eight abdominal operations and missed all but the opening game in 1964. A year of forced retirement due to his suspension for gambling had shaken Paul Hornung's confidence. A fine marksman in 1960 and 1961, Hornung made only 12 of 38 field-goal tries all year. Missed extra points caused one-point losses to the Baltimore Colts and Minnesota Vikings, and then in a rematch with Baltimore, Hornung missed five field-goal attempts in a 24–21 loss.

Lombardi, of course, knew all about the quirky, balding Chandler because he was on the Giants' coaching staff when Don was a rookie. When Lombardi swung the deal with the Giants in the spring of 1965, he knew he had his kicker.

Chandler had been with the Giants for nine years. An outstanding punter who once boomed a ball 107 yards against Dallas, he doubled as a place-kicker after Pat Summerall's retirement and set New York's scoring with 106 points in 1963. He helped the Giants win five Eastern Division championships.

Because his growing business interests in Tulsa were demanding more than off-season attention, Chandler made an unusual request of the Giants

Coach Vince Lombardi conferred with his quarterback, Bart Starr, about his game plan against the Browns. The Packers' effective running game, spiced with just enough Starr passing, gave the Packers essential ball control as they ran off 69 plays to the Browns' 39.

Bill Glass (No. 80), the Browns' 6'5" defensive end, leapt high to deflect a Bart Starr pass, but the ball already was downfield as 50,777 bundled fans watched the play on a dark and snowy day in Lambeau Field.

after the 1964 season. He asked permission to work a split week, minding business in Oklahoma and rejoining the Giants for a couple of days of practice before each game.

Coach Allie Sherman and team owner Wellington Mara flatly refused his request. "A player like that, once he gets unhappy, really should be traded," Sherman reasoned. "He will carry the resentment all season, and it could affect everyone."

The Giants unloaded Chandler to the Packers. Cheap. For a third-round draft pick.

When he arrived in Green Bay, Chandler had a long talk with Lombardi. He had hoped to convince Lombardi that he could make the same arrangement with the Packers that he had asked of the Giants. He wanted to commute between Green Bay and Tulsa during the season. Fat chance.

"I thought I had heard all the coaching speeches," Chandler said. "I was convinced of what I wanted to do, and I told him that when we first sat down.

"An hour or so later, I couldn't wait to change my plans. I'll say this about Vince Lombardi: he was hypnotic when he wanted to be. I remember the first time I sat in when he delivered one of those pregame speeches. When it was over, I was afraid to miss a field goal, not because we might lose, but because I'd have to face him afterward."

Lombardi made full use of Chandler's talents as the Packers and Baltimore Colts finished in a first place tie with 10–3–1 records in 1965. Chandler made 17 of the 26 field-goal attempts and led the team in scoring with 88 points. He also handled the punting and averaged 42.9 yards. His 90-yard punt against San Francisco still stands as a Packers record.

But nothing Chandler had accomplished would compare to what he did on the day after Christmas in Lambeau Field. In the end, when it became obvious that neither muscle nor magic would produce a winner against the Colts, Chandler stepped to the line and kicked a close-shave 27-yard field goal that sent the Western Conference playoff game into sudden-death overtime. And then he drilled home the game-winner from 25 yards after 13 minutes and 39 seconds of overtime.

The score was 13–10. A knife job. It gave the Packers the right to play host to the defending champion Cleveland Browns for the NFL title the following Sunday.

The Colts, who took the Packers down to the wire with Tom Matte at quarterback because Johnny Unitas and backup Gary Cuozzo both were injured, screamed bloody murder that Chandler's field goal, which had sent the game into the longest overtime in NFL history, clearly missed its mark. "Wide by three feet," Colts tackle Lou Michaels shouted in disbelief.

57

"During the game, I came back to the bench after scoring a touchdown and I said, 'It's just like the good old days!' Lombardi took up the cry. He said, 'Did you hear that? It's just like the good old days! Just like the good old days!'"

—PAUL HORNUNG

NFL CHAMPIONSHIP
January 2, 1966

The Green Bay Packers vs. the Cleveland Browns
Lambeau Field, Green Bay, Wisconsin
Score: Green Bay 23, Cleveland 12
Attendance: 50,777

SCORING SUMMARY:

Cleveland	9	3	0	0	- 12
Green Bay	7	6	7	3	- 23

GB: Dale 47-yard pass from Starr (Chandler kick)
Clev: Collins 17-yard pass from Ryan (kick failed)
Clev: Groza 24-yard field goal
GB: Chandler 15-yard field goal
GB: Chandler 23-yard field goal
Clev: Groza 26-yard field goal
GB: Hornung 13-yard run (Chandler kick)
GB: Chandler 29-yard field goal

The next day the Baltimore newspapers ran a picture showing the ball in the air just after it passed the goal post, and from the angle of the shot it looked as if it might have missed. The problem was that the uprights in that era were extremely short.

The next year, the league extended the uprights 20 feet above the crossbar. They were called the Chandler Extension.

Thirty-six years later, Lombardi's Packers met for a reunion in Green Bay. As they walked out on Lambeau Field to relive the glory years, one of his old teammates pointed to the goal post and yelled to 67-year-old Chandler, "Hey, Don, show us where you missed that kick."

Everyone had a good laugh, including Chandler.

"I was in Baltimore three months ago, and they're still talking about it being no good," Chandler said, his Super Bowl II ring glistening in the bright sun. "Bart Starr held the ball on that kick and he said it cleared the bar, then sailed right."

Starr agreed. "I held for kickers for years," he said. "I'd like to think I had a very good view of it. I didn't see any problem. I don't know what all the stir was about."

The Packers had paid a heavy price in eliminating the Colts. Starr was knocked out of the game on the first play of the game when Baltimore

Gary Collins was closely defended by the Packers' Bob Jeter (No. 21) and Tom Brown (No. 40) on this pass play. Collins scored the Browns' only touchdown on a 17-yard reception but caught only two more passes for 27 yards.

Jim Taylor, playing with a pulled groin muscle, found the soft and slippery turf to his liking as he was determined to run straight over the Browns. Coming up late for the tackle was Paul Wiggin (No. 84) of the Browns.

linebacker Don Shinnick scooped up a fumble and headed for the hills, and a blocker leading the way smacked Starr in the ribs. Bratkowski, who had been kicked around from Chicago to Los Angeles to Green Bay and all the points in between, took over at quarterback for the Packers.

"When Bart didn't get up, I knew I was going in," Bratkowski said. "All I remember is that I thought that now it's all up to me, all the responsibility and all the money and the championship . . . all mine. My stomach started to churn."

Bratkowski, who came to the Packers midway through the 1963 season, had convinced Lombardi that he was more than a capable backup quarterback. He had saved four games in relief of Starr in 1965, and in the showdown with the Colts he completed 22 of 39 passes for 248 yards as the Packers won and headed for the NFL championship game against the Cleveland Browns.

They were not a very impressive group as they went back to work. Foremost among the walking wounded were Starr with aching ribs; Jim Taylor with a pulled groin muscle; Boyd Dowler with a bad ankle and two damaged ribs; Paul Hornung with a twisted knee, bruised ribs, and a sprained wrist; and defensive tackle Ron Kostelnik with a sprained knee.

"There was a sign in our locker room, and I think we all knew it related to our mission, to [stopping] Jim Brown. It said, 'Pursue in the shortest course to the ball carrier. Arrive in bad humor.'"

—LIONEL ALDRIDGE

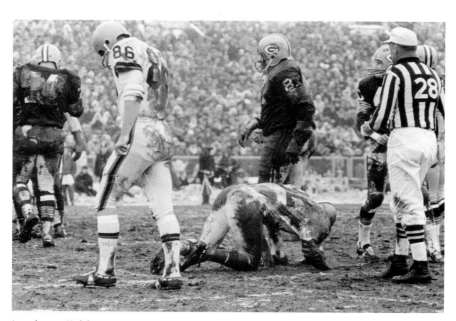

Lambeau Field was not a good place to be for Jim Brown. Merciless on defense, the Packers walked away after dumping Brown yet again in the slop while teammate Gary Collins trudged back to the Cleveland huddle.

Bart Starr enjoyed perfect protection as he threw against the Browns. Tackle Forrest Gregg (No. 75), guard Jerry Kramer (blocking Dick Modzelewski, No. 74), and Jim Taylor (No. 31, blocking Bill Glass) got the job done.

Tackle Forrest Gregg, playing in his ninth year at Green Bay, was a muddied but satisfied warrior as he came to the Packers' sideline after winning battles in the trenches against the Browns.

The only healthy thing about this team was Lombardi's appetite for another championship. He had been consumed with the idea of winning three NFL championships in a row ever since that windy December night when he and the Packers had flown home after their second title triumph over the New York Giants.

Two days before their showdown with the Browns, it was more like a day in October than late December as the Packers hustled through their last big workout under ideal conditions. The No. 1 offensive unit was intact, but Lombardi hesitated when asked about his quarterback.

"If I told you Bart was going to start I might be wrong," Lombardi told reporters. "And if I told you he wasn't going to start, I might not be telling the truth. I just won't know for sure until he warms up Sunday."

Waiting for them were the Browns and the well-rested Jimmy Brown, the most dynamic force in pro football. The big fullback had dominated

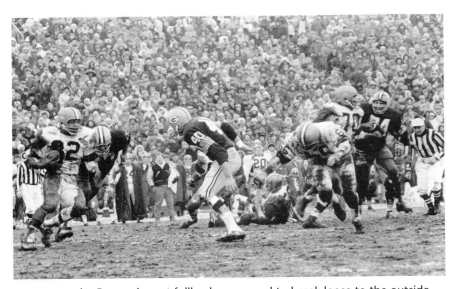

Jim Brown, the Browns' great fullback, managed to break loose to the outside before Tom Brown prepared to tackle him. Brown wound up with a skimpy 50 yards gained rushing. Green Bay linebacker Ray Nitschke was the key to stopping Brown, reading him as though Nitschke had been with him in the Cleveland huddle.

"The 1961 and 1962 teams, I believe, were a cut above everyone else. But by 1965 and in the two years after that, too, things had evened out a lot. There were four or five other teams with comparable personnel. They could have won it. The point is they didn't. We won it and I know now it was the motivation the man gave us that did it."

—BOYD DOWLER

---

the game like no other player had, winning the NFL rushing title in eight of his nine seasons. His numbers in 1965—1,544 yards, 5.3 yards per carry, and 17 touchdowns—were his best ever.

On the day before the game, Brown was in a jocular mood as he kidded with his Cleveland teammates in the visitors' locker room at Lambeau Field. The Browns' great running back primped in front of a mirror before he was to make a television appearance to receive the Jim Thorpe trophy as the NFL's biggest star.

Earlier in the week, he had expressed fear that the field in Green Bay would be frozen or snow covered and not suited for his particular talents. But after an inspection of the field Saturday, he was confident that he and the Browns would win.

There was a report that a big snowstorm was scheduled to hit the Green Bay area before Sunday. In view of the mild winter and hardly any snow on the ground, Lombardi was skeptical of the report.

"Nobody wants a bad field," he said. "But I'll guarantee the field will be ready no matter what happens."

A four-inch snowstorm hit Sunday morning. While the Lambeau Field ground crew was trying to make the field playable, the Browns were trying to make the 30-mile trip from Appleton, where they had headquartered, by bus. But the snow-covered highway, made even more treacherous by a freezing rain and bumper-to-bumper stadium traffic with cars spinning off the road, turned a normally easy drive into a one-hour-and-50-minute nightmare.

In spite of the sloppy going, Jim Taylor barged through the Browns with Paul Hornung leading the way. Taylor came up with about the best game of his career, running straight over the Browns while gaining 96 yards on 27 carries.

In Green Bay, the snow waited until the protective tarpaulin had been removed from the field in the morning and then swooped down, preceded by rain and followed by sleet, to coat the surface of the ground with a muddy grease. By game time, the field was holding up quite well until the fourth quarter, when it turned into a total quagmire.

Mark Duncan, the supervisor of officials, tried to borrow the dye used in marking the ice at hockey games from the Brown County Arena in order to define the sidelines and goals, but it didn't work. Finally, he placed small flags 10 yards apart all along the out-of-bounds line.

Jim Taylor got up at 8:00 A.M. Sunday and peered out of the window of his room at the Bay Motel. "I liked what I saw," he recalled as he dressed for the game. "I knew the snow was going to equalize some things."

Taylor and his family had moved to the motel Friday to avoid having to pay another month's rent on their leased home, and it was there Saturday

Behind a solid wall of protection, Bart Starr threw downfield against the Cleveland Browns. Knocked out in the playoff game against Baltimore with a rib injury, Starr came back against the Browns, completing 10 of 18 passes for 147 yards—including a 47-yard touchdown pass to Carroll Dale in a game played under most difficult field conditions.

The treacherous field did not slow down Paul Hornung. The Golden Boy was superb, rushing for 105 yards in 18 carries, with one burst of 34 yards.

Frank Ryan (No. 13) got adequate protection on this play. But for the most part, the Cleveland quarterback had trouble finding open receivers. Ryan completed only 8 of 18 passes for 115 yards and one touchdown and had two intercepted.

night that he first learned of the messy snowstorm that was approaching the city.

"We heard on television that the forecast was for some snow, but not this much," he said. "When I saw it this morning I knew it could only be good news."

Starr was still quite sore when Lombardi decided to start him. He wore some makeshift special rib pads that team trainer Domenic Gentile made for him, and he took shots to numb the pain.

"I wasn't quite where I wanted to be, but it was such an important game," Starr said. "They had treated me the best they could during the week. They had done all they could. I just tried to block it out and do the best I could."

It was a game played under the most difficult conditions, and maybe what happened to Starr on the Packers' first touchdown to Dale explained

SEASON RECORD

DATE	OPPONENT	W/L	GB	OPP	LOC	ATTENDANCE
9/19/65	Pittsburgh Steelers	W	41	9	Pitt	38,383
9/26/65	Baltimore Colts	W	20	17	Milw	48,130
10/3/65	Chicago Bears	W	23	14	GB	50,852
10/10/65	San Francisco 49ers	W	27	10	GB	50,852
10/17/65	Detroit Lions	W	31	21	Det	56,712
10/24/65	Dallas Cowboys	W	13	3	Milw	48,311
10/31/65	Chicago Bears	L	10	31	Chi	45,664
11/7/65	Detroit Lions	L	7	12	GB	50,852
11/14/65	Los Angeles Rams	W	6	3	Milw	48,485
11/21/65	Minnesota Vikings	W	38	13	Minn	47,426
11/28/65	Los Angeles Rams	L	10	21	LA	39,733
12/5/65	Minnesota Vikings	W	24	19	GB	50,852
12/12/65	Baltimore Colts	W	42	27	Balt	60,238
12/19/65	San Francisco 49ers	T	24	24	SF	45,710

WESTERN CONFERENCE CHAMPIONSHIP

DATE	OPPONENT	W/L	GB	OPP	LOC	ATTENDANCE
12/26/65	Baltimore Colts	W (OT)	13	10	GB	50,484

NFL CHAMPIONSHIP

DATE	OPPONENT	W/L	GB	OPP	LOC	ATTENDANCE
1/2/66	Cleveland Browns	W	23	12	GB	50,777

it all. It was a 47-yard play on which Starr admitted, "That wet ball just slipped. It squibbed off my hand when I threw it, and it never would have been a score except that Dale made it one. I threw short. Dale stopped, came back, caught it, went by [Walter] Beach when he slipped. On a day like this you need everything."

Cleveland's X-factor, as always, was Jim Brown. Quarterback Frank Ryan went to him on the Browns' first play from scrimmage, completing a pass to Brown, who gained 30 yards to the Green Bay 36. Just two plays later, Cleveland scored when Ryan hit Gary Collins on a 17-yard pass play.

The Browns had Lou Groza, who had not failed on 96 straight extra-point conversions, ready to tie it. But Bobby Franklin, the holder on kicks, failed to handle the low snap from center. Groza pounced on it and lobbed the ball to Franklin, who never had a chance to go anywhere, and it was Green Bay 7, Cleveland 6.

Ray Nitschke wanted to dominate. He wanted to come out with a doomsday sense of vengeance. There was a level of fear and wonder he wanted to establish early. He wanted the Browns to blink at what they saw. He wanted to plant the idea in their heads that however long and cold and sloppy the day might last, success was not possible.

The Packers' middle linebacker wanted what he always wanted on game day. Only this day, he wanted it more.

Don Chandler kicked a 25-yard field goal in sudden-death overtime to give the Packers a 13–10 victory over the Baltimore Colts in the Western Conference playoff game at Lambeau Field on December 26, 1965. Chandler's "close-shave" 27-yard field goal sent the game into overtime. Had it not been for Chandler, there probably would never have been a 1965 NFL title game in Green Bay, and what eventually led to an unprecedented three straight league championships by the Packers. Chandler was the lifesaver.

On Groza's missed extra point, Nitschke barreled in and smacked John Morrow on the head, causing the center's low snap. Nitschke's bigger assignment was to stop Jim Brown, and he read the Cleveland fullback's sweeps as if he were a party to the Browns huddles. Brown finished with 50 yards rushing, 44 as a pass receiver.

"Most often when we had played Cleveland we tried to hold Brown to a number," defensive end Willie Davis said. "You're never going to stop him. We tried to take away the inside plays because whenever Brown ran those inside traps and power plays he'd get seven, eight, nine yards before you could bring him down."

Vince Lombardi had his arm around his favorite player, Paul Hornung, as the game ended. Lombardi honored his stars, bringing them out one by one to the standing ovations from the exuberant home fans.

Muddied and victorious, Paul Hornung and his guardian angels, Jerry Kramer and Fuzzy Thurston, personified the Packers' fundamental football.

It was another NFL championship for Lombardi and the Packers. The Lambeau Field scoreboard showed the final score as dusk began to settle.

"The difference this time is that we got him running laterally, and the weather helped us some. All of our linebackers played well, but the middle linebacker keyed on Brown when he lined up at the fullback position. Nitschke had an outstanding game."

Later in the third quarter Nitschke stayed step-for-step with Brown for 30 yards and tipped a sure touchdown pass out of his hands. Two plays later, Groza attempted a 37-yard field goal that was blocked by Henry Jordan.

It was supposed to be a show-us-what-you-got kind of game for Jim Brown and the Cleveland Browns. But it turned out to be just another showcase for Paul Hornung and Jim Taylor. Just another case of the Packers' relentless ball control with Green Bay running 69 offensive plays to 37 for Cleveland.

Their names: Bob Skoronski, Fuzzy Thurston, Ken Bowman, Jerry Kramer, and Forrest Gregg. Their mission: punch holes in the Browns' defense so Hornung and Taylor could run to daylight. Mission accomplished.

"Our offensive line blocked so well that we were able to execute plays just as we had planned," Starr said.

On the sloppy field that helped to neutralize Brown, Hornung was able to cut and twist for 105 yards, and Taylor ran straight over the Cleveland defense for 96 yards. Everyone knew what to expect, but the Browns couldn't stop them.

What the Browns needed was a Brown County snowplow, a bazooka, or a brick wall: *something* that could stop two runaway beer trucks. That's how Hornung and Taylor looked to the Browns.

The Packers dominated the second half as their offensive line established superiority over the Browns' defense. On their first possession in the third quarter, they marched 90 yards in 11 plays. On that drive Taylor gained 25 yards on five carries, Starr completed both of his passes (12 yards to

Jim Taylor, stripped to his shoulder pads, was interviewed by Mike Christopulos of the *Milwaukee Sentinel* in the Packers' locker room after the game. There was plenty to talk about.

Paul Hornung had the attention of CBS announcer Ray Scott in the Packers' crowded locker room after the game. Waiting to be interviewed were Bart Starr (left) and Jim Taylor.

Dowler and 10 yards to Taylor), and Hornung ran for 42 yards on four trips, including a 13-yard sweep led by blockers Jerry Kramer and Forrest Gregg for a touchdown.

"We thought we were the best club," guard Fuzzy Thurston said. "I thought we were. But I wasn't sure. And to beat a good ballclub like Cleveland, you've got to be sure. So Paul came back to the huddle and he said, 'Hey, this is 1962 again.' And all at once you could feel everybody in the huddle come up. All at once we didn't just think we could win. We knew damn well we would win."

Frank Ryan, the quarterback with the doctor's degree in advanced mathematics, completed his first four passes, with the first three accounting for all of the yardage in Cleveland's first touchdown. Then he did a disappearing act.

The only chance the Browns had was to have a live throwing day and pray for turnovers. That went pffft when Ryan completed only 4 of his last

14 passes and had two interceptions and, by his own admission, said, "Don't blame Gary Collins or Paul Warfield—they got open despite all that slush. I just couldn't get the ball to them."

Lombardi paid no attention to the elements after the game than had his players during it. "We learn to play in all weather," he said.

This certainly was not Lombardi's best team in seven years at Green Bay. All season long the Packers had their difficulties. In a way they were lucky to reach the conference playoff. But once they got there, they knew exactly what to do.

Lombardi and his players looked tired in the dressing room after the game. They had given all of themselves to winning another championship.

"This is the best win I ever had," Lombardi said. "It came so hard, all year long. Everything was hard. The season. The playoff. Everything. I never worked so hard in my life for anything."

It was, as it turned out, the last great game for Lombardi's pedigree running back tandem of Taylor and Hornung. Waiting in the wings would be Donny Anderson and Jim Grabowski, the Packers' new million-dollar backfield.

And Don Chandler? He punted well, kicked off well, scored 11 points on three field goals and two extra points, and broke the Browns' last hope by getting himself run into while attempting a fourth-quarter punt. The roughing the kicker penalty gave the ball back to the Packers.

"First time in five years my uniform has been dirty," he said with a grin.

Chandler would be part of a joyride that would last two more years.

77

"In this game, when we went against Jimmy Brown, he [Lombardi] told Nitschke, 'Now this is all you've got to do. Don't watch anybody else. This is your guy.' You know that pass that Brown dropped in the end zone? He had it in his hands but Nitschke was all over him, just hustling and hollering and screaming after him."

—BOB SKORONSKI

The Cowboys had a tough time defending against Bart Starr's passing, but to
keep the Dallas defense honest the Packers' quarterback handed off to his

CHAPTER 4

THE 1966

NFL CHAMPIONSHIP GAME

It wasn't difficult to tell the haves from the have-nots in the sixties.

The Green Bay Packers were the clear favorites every time they faced the Dallas Cowboys, and they had never lost to the Cowboys in three previous regular-season games. The Packers were more experienced in big games, were mentally tougher, and had a hard-nosed coach who simply refused to accept failure.

The Cowboys had flashy quarterback Don Meredith throwing to Bob Hayes, one of the world's fastest humans. They had a solid running game with Don Perkins and Dan Reeves, and future Hall of Famers Bob Lilly and Mel Renfro to anchor the defense. And putting it all together was a brainy, egghead-type of coach named Tom Landry, who patiently drilled his intricate system of offense and defense into a winner.

Did this make the Packers nervous? It certainly should have.

This was the day for which they had waited. This was the game that would match the coaching talents of Vince Lombardi and Tom Landry in

Green Bay fans, some 3,500 strong, made themselves conspicuous by bringing their banners and signs into the Cotton Bowl. They were relegated to sit in the end zone of the 75,000-seat stadium, which was packed that day.

a championship game. This was Lombardi and his "here-we-come, try-to-stop-us" machine against Landry's complicated multiple offense and flex defense.

Eight years earlier they had worked together on the New York Giants' staff in Yankee Stadium watching the Baltimore Colts win, 23–17. It was the first time in league history that it would take a sudden-death overtime period to determine the National Football League champion.

The next year, the 45-year-old Lombardi, who had been offensive coordinator of the Giants for five years, was hired by the Packers. Given full authority as head coach and general manager, he received a five-year contract, paying $41,000 a year, to revive the 1–10–1 underachievers he inherited at Green Bay.

The Cowboys joined the NFL as an expansion team in 1960. Landry, who had been defensive coordinator of the Giants, was 35 years old when

A confident Vince Lombardi waited in the south tunnel of the Cotton Bowl as his defending NFL champion Packers were introduced before the game. Among the players visible are (from left) Jim Weatherwax, Lee Roy Caffey, Dave Robinson, Paul Hornung, Max McGee, Boyd Dowler, Bob Skoronski, and, ready to run on the field, Forrest Gregg.

Don Meredith handed off to Don Perkins, who was looking to exploit a hole in the Packers' defense. Perkins was the game's leading rusher (with 108 yards in 17 carries) and scored on a 23-yard run.

he was given a five-year contract, paying $34,500 a year, to coach the Cowboys.

They had come face-to-face for the first time in 1960, and Lombardi's Packers punched out Landry's Cowboys, 41–7, in Green Bay. It was like an older sibling taking delight in beating up his kid brother, and it continued in 1964 as Green Bay defeated Dallas, 45–21. But the following year,

Dallas was becoming much closer to challenging Green Bay, losing to the Packers, 13–3, in Milwaukee.

While Lombardi had almost instant success at Green Bay, turning the Packers into NFL champions in 1961, 1962, and 1965, Landry struggled at Dallas. His first year ended in a disastrous 0–11–1 and was followed by four more losing seasons. But in 1966 the team with a huge inferiority complex exploded with a 10–3–1 record to win the Eastern Conference title and led the NFL in scoring with 445 points while allowing only 239.

"Mental toughness is essential to success."

—VINCE LOMBARDI

These still were the Packers, however, the team that was the measuring stick for every other team in the NFL. They won 12 games and lost only twice by a total of four points. And now with one eye on their place in history and another on the Cowboys, they began their quest for a fourth league championship under the driving whip of Lombardi.

That quest actually began in Tulsa, Oklahoma, on the day after Christmas. While the Cowboys could work in the comfortable atmosphere of their own practice facility in Dallas, Lombardi, on the spur of the moment, herded the Packers from Green Bay to Tulsa in search of a warmer climate to prepare for the game. In Tulsa, he found the same thing he left in Green Bay—snow and ice.

83

Temperatures in the low 20s had turned the rain-soaked turf at Skelly Stadium, where the team had hoped to work out, into a skating rink. Players laughed at the irony of leaving the cold and snow of Green Bay to practice in "dry and warm Tulsa," but Lombardi failed to see the humor.

He managed a tight smile as he viewed the field and suggested someone ought to start shoveling the snow. He announced the Packers' practice would be closed but had a change of mind when stadium officials pointed out that some of the viewers might be persuaded to shovel snow. About 20 volunteers manned the shovels, but it appeared they were fighting a losing battle. No one thought about obtaining wheelbarrows to carry the snow away.

When the Packers' equipment arrived late, delaying the first practice, Lombardi fumed. "This is one fouled-up operation," he said, demanding to know who was responsible. He lashed out at everybody, feeling his team had not been treated with respect.

NFL CHAMPIONSHIP
January 1, 1967

The Green Bay Packers vs. the Dallas Cowboys
The Cotton Bowl, Dallas, Texas
Score: Green Bay 34, Dallas 27
Attendance: 74,152

SCORING SUMMARY:

Green Bay	14	7	7	6	- 34
Dallas	14	3	3	7	- 27

GB: Pitts 17-yard pass from Starr (Chandler kick)
GB: Grabowski 18-yard fumble return (Chandler kick)
Dal: Reeves 3-yard run (Villanueva kick)
Dal: Perkins 23-yard run (Villanueva kick)
GB: Dale 51-yard pass from Starr (Chandler kick)
Dal: Villanueva 11-yard field goal
Dal: Villanueva 32-yard field goal
GB: Dowler 16-yard pass from Starr (Chandler kick)
GB: McGee 28-yard pass from Starr (kick failed)
Dal: Clarke 68-yard pass from Meredith (Villanueva kick)

The Packers' countdown to their showdown with the Cowboys started two days later with two new developments. First, the brutal weather in Tulsa forced the Packers to conclude their Wednesday workout inside the Tulsa Exposition Center, several miles away from Skelly Stadium. The Exposition Center covered 10½ acres under a suspended roof.

But the place was locked up when the Packers' buses arrived at the gate with no security man in sight. Lombardi got hot again, but Max McGee had a suggestion. "That's OK, Bussie," the veteran end said to the bewildered bus driver. "Just back her up a bit, and then put it to the floor and we'll ram ourselves in."

Lombardi was in a foul mood all week, and the team needed someone like McGee to humor them and keep things sane.

The Exposition building was built to display heavy oil equipment. It was huge and it had a low metal ceiling. Every time someone kicked or punted the ball it would hit the low ceiling and create the sound of a giant cymbal ringing, causing Lombardi to tell the kickers to knock it off.

Because of a concrete floor, players had to wear tennis or rippled-soled shoes to prevent them from slipping. "It was like a basketball drill," defensive back Bob Jeter said. "We worked up a good sweat, but that's about all."

The defending NFL champions' appearance in Tulsa was good for the local chamber of commerce. But Lombardi didn't give a damn that the Packers became the first football team to ever work out in the Tulsa Exposition Center. The sooner he could leave Tulsa and the cold state of Oklahoma, the better.

The second development happened five days before the title game when the *Dallas Times Herald* broke the story that Lombardi was thinking of quitting as coach of the Packers. Lombardi quitting?! Steve Perkins, a

This banner was evidence that the Packers might have been first to lay claim to the title of "America's Team."

Dallas defensive tackle Jim Colvin had Bart Starr in his sight, but the Green Bay quarterback had delivered the goods. Starr had a hot hand, completing 19 of 28 passes for 304 yards and four touchdowns.

persistent sportswriter, reported that Lombardi had intimated to him on the Tulsa practice field that the answer might be yes.

The story exploded nationally. Upon returning with the team to its hotel, Lombardi was met by a horde of newsmen. Naturally, he vehemently denied everything. "I have no intention of quitting," he said, his dark eyes flashing, when asked to comment on Perkins' story. "I think he misunderstood me. I do believe the job has become more demanding, but I have no intention of quitting."

In his eighth year as both head coach and general manager at Green Bay, Lombardi had guided the Packers to an 80–25–3 record, five division titles, and three league championships. Midway through the 1965 season, the Packers announced that they had extended his contract through 1973.

"These reports seem to crop up every year," said one member of the Packers' entourage. "I can't imagine him quitting now."

Another added, "I think he's shooting for Papa Bear's record." The reference was to George Halas, who at 71 was going strong as owner and head coach of the Chicago Bears.

The preparation for the game, by both teams, was not exactly straightforward. The Packers, who had gone through this sort of thing in five of the past seven years, claimed they had never been tenser. Getting ready for their first championship game, the Cowboys tried to pretend that it was not such a big deal and assumed an air of casualness.

"Personally, I don't think our players feel nearly as much pressure as we felt before Cleveland on Thanksgiving Day," Meredith said. "That was a game we had to win so we could win another game [St. Louis] so we could be in a position to be here in the first place.

"We've been thinking about this for a long time, challenging Green Bay for the title. Our workouts have been excellent. Our preparation has never been better."

However, Meredith gave Landry and the Cowboys a frantic time early in the week when

87

"Vince would tell us, 'Boys, if you'll not settle for anything less than the best, you will be amazed at what you can do with your lives. You'll be amazed at how much you can rise in the world.' I think this consistent unwillingness to settle for anything less than excellence was the greatest thing he left with people around him."

—BART STARR

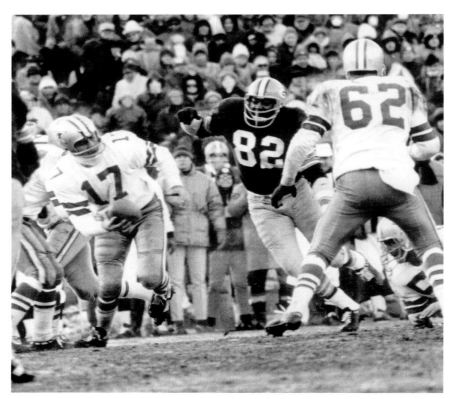

Don Meredith waited to make a handoff before getting squeezed in a Green Bay vise. Lionel Aldridge (No. 82) applied pressure on the Dallas quarterback.

he was rushed to a Dallas hospital with severe stomach cramps. It turned out to be nothing more than nerves, for the usual happy-go-lucky quarterback was wound up tighter than a drum.

The Packers were very focused on what they had to do and what they wanted to do. They were showing some age. Eleven starters were 30 or older. They were getting up there. But they were confident they would show the benefits of experience and age over unchanneled emotion.

By Friday night, after the team had flown to Dallas and had a good practice on a local high school field, Lombardi had relaxed. At his Five O'Clock Club, a traditional road game get-together with friends and media in his hotel suite, he was cheerful and smiling.

Bart Starr, the master in the clutch, delivered a pass on third and long before Dallas rushers George Andrie (No. 66) and Jim Colvin could get to him. The Packers' quarterback was not intercepted during this game.

Jim Taylor had a full head of steam as he took off here. George Andrie (No. 66) of the Cowboys looked for a would-be blocker instead of keeping his eye on the Packers' runner.

"The hay is in the barn," he said. "The team is ready. If they play as well as they know how to and lose, it will not be the end of the world. There is nothing I can do now to change anything."

Lombardi really wanted this game because to lose to Landry would have been too painful. Even when they were on the same side as top assistants with the Giants, they had been keen competitors.

"Vince had a great respect for Tom, but he always thought Tom had something up his sleeve—a secret formation, a trick play, something that he would throw at us and it would cost us the game," linebacker Dave

Robinson said. "He would get furious when Landry pulled out something new, even in the exhibition games we had against the Cowboys."

Every summer the Packers would travel to Dallas and play the Cowboys in an exhibition game in the Cotton Bowl. On the night before the game, Lombardi and his coaching staff would join Landry and his staff at Dallas owner Clint Murchison's sprawling ranch for a big-ol' Texas barbecue.

Lombardi took center stage. You could hear him all over the place. With Landry, though, you couldn't tell by looking at him whether he was having a good time or just waiting to leave. He wore the same bemused, stoic expression on his face on the sideline.

Linebacker Dave Edwards drew a bead on Jim Taylor. The Packers were outgained on the ground by the Cowboys, 187 yards to 102.

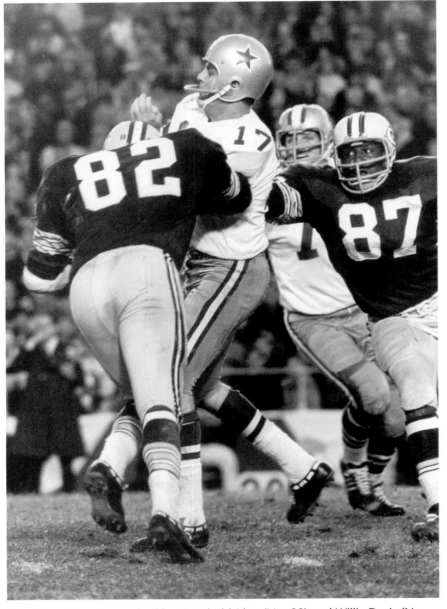

Don Meredith got crunched by Lionel Aldridge (No. 82) and Willie Davis (No. 87). The Dallas quarterback threw the ball 31 times and completed 15 passes for 231 yards, one touchdown, and one very costly interception.

"When we were leading 34–27 and Dallas had a first down on the 2-yard line, we were terrified. There was nothing we could do but pray. We hadn't stopped the Cowboys all afternoon and we knew they were going to score, and when that happened, we'd be dead. Dallas had the momentum and we were emotionally exhausted. Then somebody in the Cowboy line jumped offside and we were saved. To me, we won that game because of Vince Lombardi. Lombardi discipline was the difference. Nobody who played for Lombardi would ever have jumped offside and cost the club a ballgame or a championship. He wouldn't have permitted it."

—MAX MCGEE

93

All Landry was, was a darn good football coach. He just didn't act like it. He never misbehaved, never threw a tantrum. This really annoyed Lombardi. Landry didn't have the self-indulgent appeal of a George Halas, a Don Shula, or a Norm Van Brocklin, whom Lombardi loved to beat. Landry was a friend.

On New Year's Eve the Cowboys settled in at the Holiday Inn-Central, as they always had before a home game. Pete Gent, the tall flanker, expressed Landry's approach to the championship game. "Coach Landry has gone about this as if it were any other game," Gent said. "No trace at all of nerves or doubt. I think that is because he really believes in us and our ability; we believe in ourselves."

The point was, if the Cowboys were overachievers under Landry, they refused to concede they were over their heads against the Packers.

From a standpoint of big-game experience, this was a most unusual match. The Packers had plenty. Twelve of their players had been in four championship games since 1960. The Cowboys never had known even a winning season until now.

"It still boils down to execution," Lombardi said. "All the formations in the world won't win if you don't execute. I think we will win. In fact, I'm sure of it."

The Packers were favored by seven points to repeat as champions and represent the NFL in the first Super Bowl, to be played two weeks later in the Los Angeles Coliseum. By the time the game started, the Kansas City Chiefs already had beaten the Buffalo Bills for the American Football League championship.

The Cotton Bowl was filled nearly to its 75,000 capacity and the weather was ideal—sunny and mild—as Danny Villanueva kicked off to Herb Adderley, who returned 22 yards. On the game's first play from scrimmage, Elijah Pitts, starting for the injured Paul Hornung, burst through a hole in the Dallas defense and ran for 32 yards to the Cowboys' 44-yard line.

The play was a specially designed and disguised sucker play that, Starr recalled later, "worked just like it was designed—to take advantage of their [flex] defense."

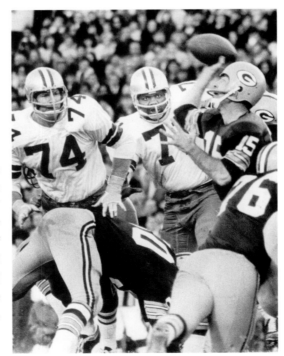

Bart Starr found enough time to throw before his pocket collapsed. Putting the pressure on the Packers' quarterback are Bob Lilly (No. 74) and Jethro Pugh of the Cowboys while Bill Curry and Bob Skoronski tried to give Starr some breathing room.

SEASON RECORD

DATE	OPPONENT	W/L	GB	OPP	LOC	ATTENDANCE
9/10/66	Baltimore Colts	W	24	3	Milw	48,650
9/18/66	Cleveland Browns	W	21	20	Cle	83,943
9/25/66	Los Angeles Rams	W	24	13	GB	50,861
10/2/66	Detroit Lions	W	23	14	GB	50,861
10/9/66	San Francisco 49ers	L	20	21	SF	39,290
10/16/66	Chicago Bears	W	17	0	Chi	48,573
10/23/66	Atlanta Falcons	W	56	3	Milw	48,623
10/30/66	Detroit Lions	W	31	7	Det	56,954
11/6/66	Minnesota Vikings	L	17	20	GB	50,861
11/20/66	Chicago Bears	W	13	6	GB	50,861
11/27/66	Minnesota Vikings	W	28	16	Minn	47,426
12/4/66	San Francisco 49ers	W	20	7	Milw	48,725
12/10/66	Baltimore Colts	W	14	10	Balt	60,238
12/18/66	Los Angeles Rams	W	27	23	LA	72,416

NFL CHAMPIONSHIP

DATE	OPPONENT	W/L	GB	OPP	LOC	ATTENDANCE
1/1/67	Dallas Cowboys	W	34	27	Dal	74,152

SUPER BOWL I

DATE	OPPONENT	W/L	GB	OPP	LOC	ATTENDANCE
1/15/67	Kansas City Chiefs	W	35	10	LA	61,946

"Actually, it was an old play, but the blocking was different," tackle Bob Skoronski added. "Vince was very good at watching film and designing a game plan. He had a great eye for that. He really could find things."

In the red formation, the Packers always swept to the right. From the brown formation, they ran the ball to the weak side. Against the Cowboys, Lombardi changed it all around.

"It was completely backwards to what the Cowboys must have expected," Skoronski said. "They had no idea what we were doing to them.

"Vince was excited all week that it was going to work, and it did. No one ever noticed the flex defense like he did. That was his baby."

Boyd Dowler was flipped by the Cowboys' Mike Gaechter as he crossed the goal line for the Packers' fourth touchdown on a 16-yard pass play in the Cotton Bowl. The Packers' flanker landed directly on his shoulder and had to be helped to the sideline by teammates Marv Fleming and Bart Starr. Starr had to pull Jim Taylor away and lead him off the field to stop him from retaliating against the Dallas safety.

The Packers were leading, 34–20, with five minutes and 20 seconds left to play, when all of a sudden Don Meredith threw a 68-yard touchdown pass to Frank Clarke to close the gap to seven points. The next time the Cowboys got the ball, Meredith had them on the move again, and on the Packers sideline (from left) Bart Starr, Paul Hornung, Zeke Bratkowski, and Vince Lombardi couldn't believe what they were seeing.

Five minutes after it began, it was 14–0. Starr connected with Pitts for a 17-yard touchdown and Chandler converted. Then Mel Renfro fumbled the kickoff, and Jim Grabowski, the rich rookie who stood in the wings waiting for Jim Taylor to tire, picked up the ball and ran 18 yards into the Dallas end zone. Chandler added the extra point.

"My feet never touched the ground," Grabowski said. "I floated back to the sidelines."

If the Cowboys had been mortally wounded, it didn't show. They came roaring back, marching 59 yards in 13 plays with Reeves running in from the Green Bay 3-yard line. Villanueva's kick made it 14–7.

Vince Lombardi, hat in hand, watched as the Cowboys' left tackle Jim Boeke jumped offside, moving Dallas back to the Green Bay 6-yard line with time running out. Max McGee said, "We won that game because of Vince Lombardi. Lombardi discipline was the difference. Nobody who played for Lombardi would ever have jumped offside and cost the club a ballgame or a championship."

Tom Brown, the Packers' strong safety, grabbed the football like a superhero catching a baby. His interception of Don Meredith's prayer in the end zone preserved the Packers' 34–27 victory.

After stopping the Packers cold on three plays and forcing them to punt, the Cowboys drove 59 yards in five plays and tied the game as Perkins broke two tackles on the way to a 23-yard touchdown. Villanueva again converted.

The 14–14 tie didn't last long. Starr found Carroll Dale with a 51-yard scoring bomb. Dale, who led all receivers with five catches for 128 yards, was covered by Cornell Green, who misjudged the ball. Dallas linebacker Lee Roy Jordan said he was so sure that Green was going to make the interception that he started to break upfield to block for him.

Two field goals by Villanueva, one before the half and one early in the third quarter, cut the Packers lead to one point, 21–20.

Now Starr, the league's MVP, was ready to cut up the Dallas secondary again. First he connected with Boyd Dowler for a 16-yard touchdown to cap a 74-yard drive in six plays. The Packers' big flanker suffered a serious shoulder injury when he was sent flying by safety Mike Gaechter's vicious hit as he crossed the Dallas goal line.

In the fourth quarter, Starr found Max McGee, who had replaced Dowler, on a 23-yard scoring play, and it gave Green Bay a commanding 34–20 lead with 5:20 left. But Chandler's extra-point attempt, his fifth, was blocked by Lilly.

For the remainder of the game it seemed the Cowboys were Meredith and Cinderella all rolled into one and multiplied by 75,000 people rocking the Cotton Bowl. Meredith began making big plays when the Cowboys needed them most.

Faced with a third down and 20 yards to go from the Dallas 32, he fired a 68-yard touchdown pass to tight end Frank Clarke, a Beloit, Wisconsin, native. Suddenly the Cowboys were back in the game. Another Dallas touchdown would tie it up.

The Packers could not move and were forced to punt back to the Cowboys. As Chandler went back to punt, Lombardi stood on the sidelines

Bart Starr, Bob Jeter, and Ben Starr (Bart's father) all had something to smile about in the Packers' locker room following the team's 34–27 victory over the Cowboys. Next was a trip to Los Angeles to meet the American Football League champion Kansas City Chiefs.

Vince Lombardi took another ride on the shoulders of his players as the Packers
left the Cotton Bowl as NFL champions for the second straight year.

and screamed, "Don't let them block it!" He expected the Cowboys to out
an all-out rush, and that's exactly what Chandler got.

He kicked hurriedly and the ball squibbed off the side of his foot and
wobbled 16 yards before going out of bounds on the Green Bay 47.
Lombardi stalked the sideline like a candidate for a straitjacket.

There was 2:50 left. It was now or never for the Cowboys, and Meredith
nearly pulled it off.

He completed a 21-yard pass to Clarke to the Green Bay 26. Then he tried
Clarke deep in the end zone, and the pass fell incomplete. But Tom Brown
was called for interference, and Dallas had the ball on the 2-yard line.

A mere two yards stood between Dallas and turning the game into a tie.
Two yards!

But against the Packers' defense, those two yards might as well have
been two miles.

Reeves made one yard, and then Meredith may have outsmarted himself. Instead of sending Perkins or Reeves up the middle again, he chose to

roll out. Dallas left tackle Jim Boeke rose up too quickly, and the Cowboys were penalized for a false start and were back on the Green Bay six.

Knowing that he would not be able to gain six yards on the ground against the Packers' defense, Meredith threw a swing pass to Reeves, but it was wide of its target. On third down, he hit tight end Pettis Norman for four yards.

Only a fourth down remained, and the Cowboys were still two yards away from sudden death. Meredith called an option play for himself. If the defense came up, he would throw; if it dropped back, he would run.

Hayes was sent in as a tight end, a position he seldom played. The idea was to isolate him on a cornerback, after he faked a block on Robinson. If Dallas could make the Packers think a sweep was coming, the cornerback would have to force the play by moving up to the line. Then Meredith would lob a short pass over his head and—if all went well—into Hayes' arms.

Robinson went right for Meredith with the snap of the ball. Hayes merely brushed him, and Meredith hardly could raise his arm before the Packers linebacker smashed into him. In desperation and off balance, Meredith threw a prayer into the end zone.

103

Brown, the Packers' strong-side safety, grabbed the football like a superhero catching a baby to preserve Green Bay's 34–27 victory. It was a catch that shocked 75,000.

In the winners' locker room, Robinson happily explained his game-saving play: "I got a good grip on Meredith's left arm and part of his right arm when he got rid of the ball. I got sick to my stomach when he got the pass off. Meredith and I were falling when he got the ball off—sort of side arm, and I could not see what was happening. The first thing I heard was the crowd. I jumped up and saw Brown getting up with the ball."

Lombardi and his teammates celebrated Robinson's heroics. Privately, the coach, the perfectionist, singled out the linebacker for an incorrect procedure on the play. He said Robinson first should have forced through the guard hole, to make Meredith hold back on his rollout plane, thus breaking up the flow of the play.

"Vince knew what I did was successful," Robinson said later. "But he would never say that. He graded everyone's performance with pluses or minuses. He gave me a minus two on the play."

Willie Davis made sure Kansas City receiver Otis Taylor was not going to take off after catching a pass from Len Dawson. Taylor, the Chiefs' best receiver, ended up with four receptions for 57 yards.

CHAPTER 5

1967:

THE FIRST SUPER BOWL

This was the day when it all began.

This was the first meeting between the two rival leagues following the merger, a game arranged in 26 days because of political and legal wrangling. This was before the National Football League discovered Roman numerals.

This was the showdown between the Green Bay Packers, standard-bearers of the established NFL, and the Kansas City Chiefs, representing the upstart American Football League. This was called the AFL-NFL World Championship Game. Not the Super Bowl.

This was the game that got huge television coverage because it was a CBS-NBC playoff as well. One of the terms of the merger was that CBS, which carried NFL games, and NBC, which showed the AFL, both got to carry this one.

This was the game when each team used its own league ball on offense. This was the strangest of all championship games.

Frank Gifford of CBS did a live, on-the-field interview with Vince Lombardi before the game. Gifford later disclosed that during the five-minute interview, Lombardi kept holding on to him and was "shaking like hell."

The Packers were 13½-point favorites to win it. They had captured the NFL title for the fourth time in six years under Vince Lombardi, defeating the Dallas Cowboys, 34–27, in the Cotton Bowl. They were a dominating team created in the image of their coach.

The Chiefs had won the AFL championship by blowing out the Buffalo Bills, 31–7, and Hank Stram, their bantam-rooster coach, let himself get carried away by the wonder of it all. "Pour it on, boys," he chirped as he watched the rout in Buffalo. "There will be a lot more when we tear apart the NFL."

Although ticket sales ($6, $10, and $12) were slow, Commissioner Pete Rozelle predicted the game would sell out. It did not. Despite sunny skies and a delightful 72-degree day at the Los Angeles Memorial Coliseum, only 61,946 fans showed up, leaving one-third of the stadium empty and the game blacked out in the Los Angeles area.

Lombardi might have helped drum up interest in the game if he had brought his team to Los Angeles the week before the game as Rozelle had asked him to do. He refused, citing too many distractions in Tinseltown. He wanted to take the Packers to Palo Alto, 400 miles north. Palo Alto was his favorite training site when the team traveled to the West Coast to play the San Francisco 49ers and the Los Angeles Rams.

Rozelle demanded the Packers set up camp in the Los Angeles area. Lombardi didn't back down. They went back and forth, and a compromise was reached. Sort of.

The Packers stayed in Santa Barbara, a beautiful coastal resort city about 90 miles north of Los Angeles. But when Lombardi got off the team bus from the airport and looked at the majestic mountains that surrounded the plush Santa Barbara Inn and the oceanfront view, his face dropped.

This was not what he had expected. This was a luxurious resort, a vacation haven. Lombardi wanted something barren. He would correct things in a hurry. Forget the beautiful surroundings, he would make it like training camp all over again. It would be like preparing for their most hated rivals—the Chicago Bears.

There would be no distractions. He made sure every minute was mapped out. The players had no time for themselves.

He took care of any extra time by telling them things like, "I want all players on the bus parked near the main lobby at nine-thirty in the morning. Do you hear me? Nine-thirty in the morning."

Len Dawson tried to find an open receiver in the Green Bay defense. The Kansas City quarterback completed 16 of 27 passes for 211 yards, but he directed only one touchdown drive.

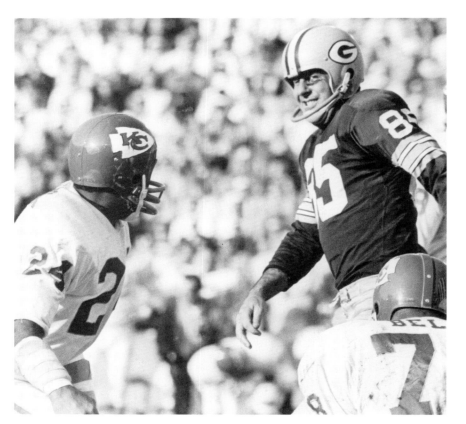

Max McGee, a 12-year veteran who didn't expect to play, flashed a smile at Chiefs' defensive back Fred Williamson after catching a Bart Starr pass for a 37-yard touchdown. Filling in for the injured Boyd Dowler, McGee turned seven of Starr's passes into 138 yards and two touchdowns.

So all the players got there at 9:15, grabbed a seat on the bus and were ready to go to practice. But Lombardi told the driver not to leave until 10:00. It was his way of using up 45 minutes of their time.

"He told us this game was so big that if anything went wrong he would fine us $2,500 for a minor violation, such as being late for a meeting, and $5,000 for a major violation, like being caught for sneaking past curfew," Packers linebacker Dave Robinson said. "That was unheard of."

That was real money in a time when $25,000 a year made a Pro Bowl player like Robinson happy. It was an indication of how seriously Lombardi took the game.

"Bart hit third down after third down pass to Max McGee because they covered the strong side and Max was just standing there. Bart just threw and threw and threw to him. And that goes along with coach Lombardi's theory. He demanded that you throw the ball. He didn't care. When the linebacker is inside and rolls in, you throw the ball. He didn't care if it was third and 1 or whatever, just throw the ball because he knew your percentage was going to be high. He expected it to be high, he demanded it be high. And so the receivers knew. When they saw the linebackers inside, they expected the automatic. That's the way it was with McGee all day."

—ZEKE BRATKOWSKI

Bob Hope was among the Hollywood celebrities attending the first Super Bowl (though it wasn't called that) in the Los Angeles Coliseum. There was plenty of room because a surprisingly small crowd of only 61,946 turned out in the huge stadium, which was one-third empty.

SUPER BOWL I
January 15, 1967

The Green Bay Packers vs. the Kansas City Chiefs
Memorial Coliseum, Los Angeles, California
Score: Green Bay 35, Kansas City 10
Attendance: 61,946

SCORING SUMMARY:

Kansas City	0	10	0	0 - 10
Green Bay	7	7	14	7 - 35

GB: McGee 37-yard pass from Starr (Chandler kick)
KC: McClinton 7-yard pass from Dawson (Mercer kick)
GB: Taylor 14-yard run (Chandler kick)
KC: Mercer 31-yard field goal
GB: Pitts 5-yard run (Chandler kick)
GB: McGee 13-yard pass from Starr (Chandler kick)
GB: Pitts 1-yard run (Chandler kick)

"He was pretty adamant that we were not going to let the NFL down," Red Cochran, backfield coach on Lombardi's staff, said. "There was no way we were going to lose this game.

"He wanted to make sure we were going to play the game at the height of our efficiency. He felt if we did that, we were going to win. You never did catch any thought of desperation that there was a chance that they were going to be so good that we couldn't beat them. He just wanted to make sure that we were ready to play a good game."

In 1967, the National Football League *was* professional football, and the mighty Green Bay Packers *were* the NFL, and Vince Lombardi *was* the Packers. Who better to carry the establishment banner against what many people considered the Mickey Mouse American Football League?

The Chiefs set up headquarters in nearby Long Beach. Hank Stram had actually made hotel arrangements for this game before the AFL title game in Buffalo. He was that confident the Chiefs could beat the Bills, and when that was accomplished it meant a two-week stay in Long Beach waiting for the Packers.

Stram tried to keep his players loose. He worked the humiliation angle. He had a recording of the Mickey Mouse Club song played when the team went on the field, and he issued Mouseketeer caps to the players.

The Chiefs coach figured the parody could create one of two reactions. "It could keep us loose and relaxed, or it could make us determined to play harder," he said.

Lombardi was on edge all week in Santa Barbara. He was carrying the weight of the entire NFL. The telegrams were arriving from the other NFL teams. They all said pretty much the same thing: "Go out there and show those clowns who's boss."

Lombardi had never seen an AFL game. Preoccupied with the Cowboys, he did not turn his thoughts to the Chiefs until after the NFL championship game in Dallas. He sent scout Wally Cruice to Buffalo, but when the Packers started preparation for the Chiefs, he ruefully admitted that he wished he knew more about them.

Buck Buchanan, the biggest player in the game, walked off the field dejectedly after a long day. The Chiefs' 6'7", 287-pound right tackle had prepared all week, studying his opponent, Fuzzy Thurston, the Packers' stubby left guard. Thurston said Buchanan's big problem would be finding him.

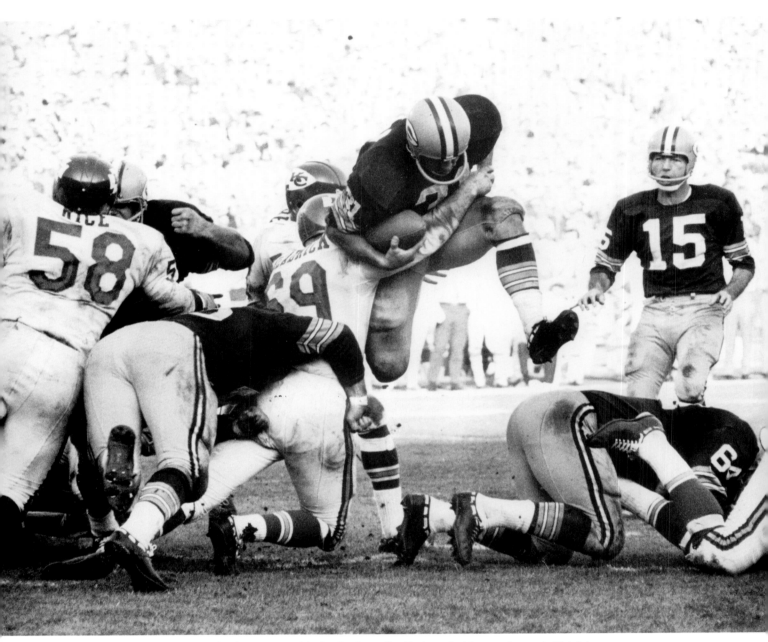

Playing his last game with the Packers, Jim Taylor tried to run through Chiefs' linebacker Sherrill Headrick. The veteran fullback carried the ball 16 times for 53 yards. The following season, Taylor played for the New Orleans Saints.

"What I know of their personnel is from information I gathered from player drafts and from films of the Chiefs' last three games," he said. "They've got some excellent athletes—players who were first- and second-round draft choices by the National Football League. You can go right down their roster: Mike Garrett, Curtis McClinton, Otis Taylor, Chris Burford—they are all top athletes."

He added, however, that everything was relative and that it was difficult to evaluate the Chiefs because the Packers were unfamiliar with the teams they played in the AFL. Reminded that even Rozelle had seen the other league play, Lombardi replied, "Pete has a lot more free time than I do."

The Packers realized the magnitude of this first AFL-NFL World Championship Game when television crews from the two networks began converging on them. The Santa Barbara Inn looked like a Hollywood studio as CBS and NBC fought for player interviews. Never had there been such ballyhoo before a pro football game. They were everywhere, hovering

"Super Sights and Sounds" was the theme of the entertainment at the game; Dixieland trumpet star Al Hirt took center stage.

around like fruit flies—digging, always digging. For an angle, a quote, a fact, a crumb, an outlandish request.

"It became absolutely ridiculous," Packers publicity director Chuck Lane said. "It was head-on competition with their promotion departments working at it full time. One network asked me if I would mind asking coach Lombardi to pose with some of his players on a trampoline. I said damn right I'd mind asking coach Lombardi to pose with some of his players on a trampoline. I wasn't about to let Lombardi kill me."

Linebacker Lee Roy Caffey lunged to tackle Chiefs' runner Bert Coan, who lost four yards on the play.

Cool, calm, and collected, Bart Starr attempted another pass; the Chiefs' Jerry Mays couldn't get close to him. Starr passed for 250 yards and two touchdowns and was named the game's most valuable player.

Marie Lombardi traveled to all the games with her husband, and she always was there with him at the Five O'Clock Club in their hotel suite. He wanted her there. Lombardi was so obsessed in his preparation for the game that she left for Las Vegas for two days and he hardly noticed she was gone.

Super Bowl I was televised by two networks: CBS, which covered the NFL, and NBC, which covered the AFL. Two of the commentators, Paul Christman (left) of NBC and Frank Gifford of CBS, met on the field before the game.

"You mean you flew over the mountains?" he said to her when she got back. "No dummy, I flew under them," she replied, drawing laughs from everyone in the room but Lombardi. If anyone could put down Vince, it was Marie.

Lombardi wasn't having the time of his life. He didn't know much about the Chiefs. He just knew he was expected to put a whipping on them.

But a cornerback named Fred Williamson made Lombardi's day. Williamson, who boasted a black belt in karate, issued a warning to the Packers: he said he possessed a secret weapon called "the Hammer," a hard forearm chop across the helmet. He vowed he would drop it on the Packers and take them out single-handedly if he had to. He would be the only player wearing white shoes because he wanted to be seen.

The only laughs the Packers had all week was when they read the papers and saw what Williamson had to say.

"Everybody was laughing at him," Packers guard Fuzzy Thurston said. "What a goofball. He kept yakking all week. Nobody was concerned about him."

Quarterback Len Dawson tried to roll out against the onrushing Willie Davis. In the second half, Lombardi told his defense to put more pressure on Dawson and create some opportunities for the offense.

Thurston was more concerned about No. 86, Buck Buchanan, the Chiefs' 6'7", 287-pound defensive tackle. Buchanan had obtained a copy of Vince Lombardi's book, *Run to Daylight*, and studied the paragraphs devoted to Thurston. Whatever thoughts Buchanan had about Thurston, he kept them to himself.

"He's about the biggest I ever played against," the Packers' stumpy guard said. "His big trouble is going to be finding me when we line up against each other. Maybe he will trip over me."

On the eve of the game, after the Packers had moved down to LA, Max McGee was ready for some action. He told Paul Hornung that he had met a couple of American Airlines stewardesses in the bar and they had agreed to meet later that night. He wanted his roommate to join him.

"He had met someone and had fallen hopelessly in love. I didn't go because I was getting married," Hornung said later. "I didn't want to get caught three days before I got married."

Linebacker Lee Roy Caffey talked to a subdued Paul Hornung, the only Packer not to get in the game. Hornung had a pinched nerve in his neck at midseason and hadn't played in six weeks.

Donny Anderson was wrapped up by the Chiefs' Bobby Ply No. 14) and Bud Abel (No. 52). Anderson carried the ball only four times and picked up 30 yards.

Their room was checked at 11:00 P.M. by Hawg Hanner, an assistant coach who was in charge of curfew bed check that night. McGee, under the covers with his coat and tie on, asked his old teammate if he was going to check his room again. Hanner said he was going to check them every hour. As he closed the door, Hawg looked back one last time and said "no." McGee was out in a flash.

"I told these two young ladies that Hornung and I would come back," McGee said. "Neither of us figured to play in the game. Then Hornung backed out because he had more value for money. The fine was something like $15,000 if you got caught breaking curfew the night before the game. Hell, that's what we were going to get if we won the game. You know, money didn't mean much to me.

"So I snuck out the back door of the hotel, got a cab, and went back to the bar where I met these young ladies. After the bar closed around 2:30, we all went to their room. I got back to my room at 7:30. I asked Hornung if they had caught me going out, and he said they did. He was lying."

Vince Lombardi conferred with his defensive coordinator, Phil Bengtson. The Packers led, 14–10, at halftime, and Lombardi ordered the blitz against Chiefs' quarterback Len Dawson. The strategy worked when Willie Wood intercepted Dawson's pass and returned it 50 yards to the Kansas City 5, where Elijah Pitts scored on the next play; the game was theirs.

McGee returned just in time for the team's breakfast. He napped for an hour and then boarded the team bus for the Coliseum.

As the game began, McGee, who had caught only four passes all season as a backup, and Hornung, sidelined for much of the regular season with a serious neck injury, were sitting on the Packers' bench. They were making plans for Hornung's wedding later that month in Hollywood, and McGee was going to throw a bachelor's party for him in Las Vegas. They were hardly paying any attention to the game.

On the second play of the game, Elijah Pitts (Hornung's replacement) ran a play around left end. When Boyd Dowler attempted to block out E. J. Holub, a Kansas City linebacker, he reinjured his shoulder and was forced to leave the game.

Lombardi screamed: "McGee! Get in there."

McGee? The 34-year-old veteran was startled. He couldn't find his helmet.

"I forgot to bring it out, and I played the first series with somebody else's helmet," he said. "I told Dad Braisher [equipment manager] to go find my helmet, and he found it."

McGee said he had absolutely no idea at first why Lombardi called him to replace Dowler.

"I hadn't played all year," he said. "Let's put it this way. He had several guys he could have put in there. I knew enough about Vince to know that he wasn't going to put in younger guys if he could stick me in there for a game that meant more to him than any game he ever coached.

"The most embarrassing thing in his career was to get beat by the AFL, and he coached accordingly. We played first to win the game and second to run up the score if we could. He would have liked to beat them 70–0."

For all of his talents and experience, McGee was like the car your aunt drives only to church on Sundays. Underused. He couldn't wait to test a Kansas City secondary that he had seen on film and played man-to-man coverage the entire game.

McGee showed his pedigree. On the Packers' second series, he ran an inside move on Chiefs' cornerback Willie Mitchell, who dove frantically in

121

"My happiest memory of him is after we won that first Super Bowl out in Los Angeles. He was really pleased. That was the last game I played for him."

—JIM TAYLOR

Max McGee scored his second touchdown to give the Packers a commanding 28–10 lead in the third quarter. The play came on third down from the Chiefs' 13-yard line. McGee was open all day, and Bart Starr just kept throwing to him.

SEASON RECORD

DATE	OPPONENT	W/L	GB	OPP	LOC	ATTENDANCE
9/10/66	Baltimore Colts	W	24	3	Milw	48,650
9/18/66	Cleveland Browns	W	21	20	Cle	83,943
9/25/66	Los Angeles Rams	W	24	13	GB	50,861
10/2/66	Detroit Lions	W	23	14	GB	50,861
10/9/66	San Francisco 49ers	L	20	21	SF	39,290
10/16/66	Chicago Bears	W	17	0	Chi	48,573
10/23/66	Atlanta Falcons	W	56	3	Milw	48,623
10/30/66	Detroit Lions	W	31	7	Det	56,954
11/6/66	Minnesota Vikings	L	17	20	GB	50,861
11/20/66	Chicago Bears	W	13	6	GB	50,861
11/27/66	Minnesota Vikings	W	28	16	Minn	47,426
12/4/66	San Francisco 49ers	W	20	7	Milw	48,725
12/10/66	Baltimore Colts	W	14	10	Balt	60,238
12/18/66	Los Angeles Rams	W	27	23	LA	72,416

NFL CHAMPIONSHIP

DATE	OPPONENT	W/L	GB	OPP	LOC	ATTENDANCE
1/1/67	Dallas Cowboys	W	34	27	Dal	74,152

SUPER BOWL I

DATE	OPPONENT	W/L	GB	OPP	LOC	ATTENDANCE
1/15/67	Kansas City Chiefs	W	35	10	LA	61,946

an effort to knock the ball away. McGee reached back with one hand, grabbed Starr's pass, and sprinted in for the 37-yard touchdown.

The message was as subtle as a punch in the jaw. The Packers had exposed a glaring weakness in the Kansas City defense.

Here was the Packers' oldest receiver announcing, "You ain't see nothin' yet," and he meant it. McGee was flat-out awesome, catching seven passes for 138 yards and two touchdowns.

It didn't surprise the Packers. "Max's experience and ability to rise to the occasion was evident," Starr said, recalling all the big pass plays he had run with McGee. "He ran patterns extremely well. He would set the defender up, and when he made his break, he could get separation from him. It was very easy to complete passes to him because of the way he ran his routes."

Hornung put it this way: "Max should have been named player of the game. I told Bart [named MVP] that a hundred times, and he agreed with me. That was the greatest performance by a guy who was out of shape. If Max had not been such a great athlete, he would never had done what he did."

"Success demands singleness of purpose."

—VINCE LOMBARDI

Everything the Chiefs heard coming to Los Angeles was run, run, run. Everyone thought the Packers were going to come out running the ball down the Chiefs' throats.

Early in the second quarter Starr had pretty well decided what he could do to Kansas City. The Packers had made a living in the NFL on short yardage situations by faking the ball to a running back going into the line and then throwing long.

Now, Starr tried it again. As Taylor made his fake into the line, Williamson came up hard—too hard. Carroll Dale raced past the suckered cornerback and was wide open when he caught Starr's pass on a shocking play that covered 64 yards and another touchdown.

The play was called back because of an illegal procedure penalty. But it was clear that the Kansas City secondary was going to be a welcome mat for the Packers' receivers. Starr put on quite a show, completing 16 of 23 passes for 250 yards and two touchdowns.

At the same time, the Chiefs were having some success cracking the Green Bay defense. They sent five receivers (including backs) out on most passing plays, leaving an unprotected Len Dawson throwing on the run.

The Chiefs drove 66 yards in six plays, scoring when Dawson hit Curtis McClinton from the Green Bay seven. The Packers went ahead on Jim Taylor's 14-yard run and Don Chandler's conversion, but their lead at halftime was trimmed to 14–10 as Mike Mercer kicked a 31-yard field goal for the Chiefs.

The Packers' defense was all worked up in the locker room. The players didn't like the way Phil Bengtson's game plan was working to the Chiefs' advantage.

"We kept complaining the whole first half that the Chiefs were getting too many guys open on passes," Robinson said. "They were running

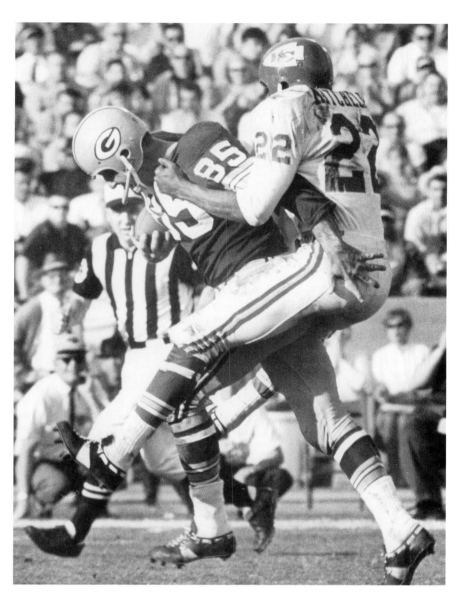

Max McGee, who wasn't supposed to play, took Willie Mitchell for a piggyback ride after catching another pass from Bart Starr. McGee reached the Kansas City 18 to set up the Packers' final touchdown in the fourth quarter. The Chiefs' young cornerback became so wary of McGee that he played well off him and became gun-shy.

five-man patterns. There was nobody back there to block for Dawson. We didn't blitz at all the first half."

Bengtson, the Packers' defensive coordinator, said he would solve that. He said the first time the Chiefs were in a pass situation, the Packers would go after Dawson.

On the fourth play of the second half, when the Chiefs had reached their 49-yard line, the Packers came with their first blitz. They sent outside line-backers Lee Roy Caffey and Robinson in with the wave of the defensive line.

Taken by surprise, Dawson was hit as he released the ball, and he threw a desperation flutterball in the general direction of tight end Fred Arbanas. But free safety Willie Wood got there first, made the interception, and picked his way 50 yards to the Kansas City 5. Pitts scored on the next play, and the Packers stretched their lead to 21–10.

Coach Hank Stram, who had predicted his Chiefs would tear apart the Packers, sang a different tune in Kansas City's losing locker room.

NFL Commissioner Pete Rozelle presented the first World Professional Football Championship Trophy to Vince Lombardi.

Faster than the Chiefs could say "gulp," the game completely turned.

The Kansas City offense totaled 12 yards in the third quarter, while the Packers scored twice, turning the game into a rout. On a 56-yard drive, Starr hit McGee three times—for 11, 16, and 13 yards. McGee juggled the last one before hauling it in one-handed in the end zone.

The Hammer? In the fourth quarter, the Packers ran a sweep with Donny Anderson carrying the ball and Gale Gillingham leading interference. Williamson went into the Packers' rookie guard low, was knocked out cold, and was carried off the field.

"I hit him with my knee," Gillingham said, laughing. "He caught it flush on the head. It's ironic. He was supposed to be the one knocking everybody out, and he's the one who is knocked out."

"He could have made a success out of the Edsel."

—SONNY JURGENSEN

CBS announcer Pat Summerall interviewed Paul Hornung before turning to Elijah Pitts (left) and Willie Wood. Although he suited up for what would be his last appearance with the Packers, Hornung never got into the game because of a neck injury.

Williamson played for only one more season, but he did later go to Hollywood and became a movie actor.

In the winners' dressing room after their 35–10 victory, Lombardi was continuously questioned by reporters about how the two leagues differed.

Finally, Lombardi said, "Kansas City has a good team. But they don't even rate with some of the teams in the NFL. Dallas is a better team. That's what you want me to say, isn't it? There. I've said it."

That same night, the Packers boarded their chartered plane at LA International to return to Green Bay. A dense fog prevented them from leaving, and so they had their victory dinner in the grounded plane.

Then they boarded buses to take them back to the Stardust Hotel near the airport, an available place Milwaukee travel agent Tom Kaminski found on the spur of the moment. Needless to say, the world champions celebrated in near obscurity.

The next day Max McGee made headlines in the morning papers. He was the toast of the sporting world. And Lombardi, according to Max, never knew he had snuck out and stayed out the night before the big game.

"Until he died, I never talked about it because I didn't want him to know," McGee said later. "I wanted him to know that he always had control of his boys.

"Sometimes I think the emphasis of sneaking out is a little overrated. The next day don't bother you. It's the day after that.

"I just went out and had a little fun. I might have taken a little nap in those girls' room. I don't remember. I was obviously ready to play football."

McGee announced his retirement after the game. He had a lot of business deals cooking and didn't need football. Lombardi told him to come back for another season. If he did not make the team, Lombardi intended to add him to his coaching staff at his current player salary.

Coach McGee?

"I knew a lot about the game," he said. "It came easy for me. I don't think I could have taught somebody. I would never have been a good coach. If you look at good coaches, I had none of those characteristics."

As it turned out, McGee returned for his 12th season at Green Bay. He got to play in another Super Bowl and catch a final pass—for 35 yards.

"The thing I remember most about him is that he was very much interested in the total man as far as his players were concerned. In other words, that we be not only good football players and winners, but that we be citizens the town would be proud of. He also taught us unselfishness and brotherly love. Those are the very words he used."

—CARROLL DALE

129

Finally relaxed and happy, Vince Lombardi left the field after his Packers deflated the Chiefs, 35–10. The long season had ended and, once again, nobody was better than the Packers.

On a frozen field against an ice-hard Dallas defense, Bart Starr (No. 15) scored with only 13 seconds to play, leading the Green Bay Packers to a 21–17 victory and the NFL championship for the third straight year. Guard Jerry Kramer (No. 64) and center Ken Bowman (under the pile) provided the blocks Starr needed to wedge into the end zone. Chuck Mercein raised his arms to show officials he hadn't pushed Starr, which would have been a penalty.

CHAPTER 6

THE 1967
NFL CHAMPIONSHIP GAME

As long as people pay attention to pro football, they will talk about what happened on New Year's Eve, 1967, at Lambeau Field.

Folks may have to look up the final score: Green Bay 21, Dallas 17.

But they will remember the Packers driving on the frozen tundra with fewer than five minutes remaining in the game.

They will remember Bart Starr scoring the winning touchdown on a daring quarterback sneak from the Dallas 1-yard line at the end of a game that seemed utterly hopeless.

And, surely, they will remember the weather.

It was the coldest New Year's Eve in Green Bay's cold history.

It was 13 below zero at the start of the 1967 National Football League championship game with northwest winds gusting up to 30 miles per hour making it feel like 49 below. Now that's cold.

The league was concerned about whether to play the game or not. But let's be realistic. How do you postpone an NFL championship game? When

A Packer Backer displayed his thoughts for everyone to see at Lambeau Field. It was a day and a game that the capacity crowd would remember forever.

would you replay it? The next day, when the weather might be even worse in Green Bay, known this January as the North Pole?

Around here, they make no bones over the fact that cold weather is Packer weather—and the colder the better. But this was ridiculous.

"You just don't play football in temperatures like that," Dallas coach Tom Landry said later. At least three Cowboys suffered frostbite and two others had medical treatment for exposure to the arctic conditions.

"I damn near froze my toes off," Packers middle linebacker Ray Nitschke said. "It was a miserable feeling."

Nitschke suffered severe frostbite, as did several of his teammates. Vince Lombardi said only the Cowboys got frostbite.

"Nitschke just had a blister," Lombardi said. "Only a blister. That's all it was. A blister."

The game is a part of Green Bay's rich football history. It has become a legend of the city. The Ice Bowl.

Over the years at least half a million people have claimed to have been in Lambeau Field the day the Packers drove 68 yards in 12 plays on the frozen field to beat the Cowboys and win a trip to Super Bowl II.

"Were you in Lambeau Field that day, Grandpa?"

"Damn right I was."

"Tell me about it."

Donny Anderson drew the pursuit of Cowboys Cornell Green (No. 34) and Chuck Howley as he ran for a first down on the frozen field. Anderson was a key player in the Packers' victory, rushing for 35 yards in 18 carries and catching four passes for 44 yards.

Don Perkins was a sitting duck as five Green Bay defenders—(from left) Tom Brown, Henry Jordan, Lee Roy Caffey, Ray Nitschke, and Willie Wood—converged on him.

"Well, you see, there were 16 seconds to play, the Packers were on the Dallas 1-yard line. Nobody left the stadium. It came down to the last play, and it looked bad for us, boy, real bad . . ."

Willie Davis didn't see it. On the Packers' bench, the big defensive end was thinking of all the things that could possibly go wrong as Starr lined up to call the last play. He couldn't watch.

"I turned around and looked up in the stands," he admitted later. "I was thinking if this was going to be the end of our great run, I didn't want to witness it at that moment. I had eye contact with this one guy in the stands. He went from a blank stare to a guy who suddenly leaped in the air and raised his arms in victory. Then I knew good stuff had happened. I had no idea if it had been a quarterback sneak or what."

Leading 17–14 with 16 seconds to play, the Cowboys would have left Green Bay as NFL champions if they had stopped Starr on the 1-yard line. Ironically, one year earlier, in Dallas, the Cowboys were down on the Packers' 2-yard line in the closing moments and couldn't score and lost, 34–27. The Cowboys wanted the Packers real bad.

Age was creeping up on the Packers. They had endured an injury-riddled season and finished 9–4–1. They made the playoffs only because the league had expanded to four divisions prior to the 1967 season.

135

Did it really happen again? Who but the man in the moon would believe Lombardi would gamble and go for the win instead of kicking a field goal to tie the game and send it into sudden-death overtime? Was that really Bart Starr scoring on a quarterback sneak? Had it all been a mass hallucination?

If it was a dream, nobody among the half-frozen capacity crowd of 50,861 in Lambeau Field wanted that special moment to end. After storming the field and tearing down the metal goal posts as if they were matchsticks, they headed home as fast as they could to thaw out and celebrate the New Year like no other.

"I ran into Willie Davis in the lobby of the Northland that morning. I said, 'Man, it's going to be cold out there,' and he said, 'Yeah,' and blew on his hands. He had gloves on and he said, 'I sure wish the man would let me wear these today.' I said, 'Aw, he'll let you wear 'em today.' Willie said, 'No way.'"

—JIM KENZIL

Commissioner Pete Rozelle wasn't at the game. He was 2,000 miles west and 80 degrees warmer in Oakland, watching the Raiders wrap up the AFL championship by whipping the Houston Oilers, 40–7.

NFL CHAMPIONSHIP
December 31, 1967

The Green Bay Packers vs. the Dallas Cowboys
Lambeau Field, Green Bay, Wisconsin
Score: Green Bay 21, Dallas 17
Attendance: 50,861

SCORING SUMMARY:

Dallas	0	10	0	7	- 17
Green Bay	7	7	0	7	- 21

GB: Dowler 8-yard pass from Starr (Chandler kick)
GB: Dowler 43-yard pass from Starr (Chandler kick)
Dal: Andrie 7-yard fumble return (Villanueva kick)
Dal: Villanueva 21-yard field goal
Dal: Rentzel 50-yard pass from Reeves (Villanueva kick)
GB: Starr 1-yard run (Chandler kick)

Contacted by the *Dallas Times Herald* to comment on the Green Bay/Dallas game, Rozelle said he preferred playing the NFL title game in a warm climate and on a neutral field. "I'm for it," Rozelle told the Dallas paper. "I'll work to get it moved. Under the conditions it was played [in Green Bay], the game is unfair to both teams."

Tex Schramm, president and general manager of the Cowboys, was even more adamant about the playing conditions in Green Bay. "It's unfortunate from the Packers' standpoint that the two most crucial games they played this year [Los Angeles in Milwaukee, December 23, and Dallas the next week in Green Bay] were not played under proper conditions," Schramm said. "This leaves everybody wondering whether the best team is representing the NFL in the Super Bowl."

Schramm said he was in no way criticizing Lombardi or his football team, adding that Vince was the only person in the league who did try to do something about it. Lombardi had installed an $80,000 electrical grid-

Dan Reeves was about to be stopped cold by Willie Wood. Reeves gained 42 yards in 13 carries against the Packers.

work under the turf at Lambeau Field to heat the ground and prevent freezing up even in extreme cold.

Lombardi bought the system from George S. Halas. No, not *that* George Halas, but a nephew of Papa Bear who was the central district sales representative for General Electric's wiring services department. Green Bay fans

"The thing that develops character in people most times is adverse situations. In other words, the discipline and conditioning programs they went through, the punishment and suffering, they all tend to develop character. And once you get character then you develop hope in all situations. That is the great thing that comes out of it. And Vince developed a lot of character in his players, character that a lot of them probably would never have had without the leadership and discipline he developed in them."

—TOM LANDRY

wondered how in the world the Packers could do business with a Halas when the Chicago Bears coach did not invest in the heating system himself.

This was the first big test for the "electric blanket."

"Lombardi was a great gadget guy," Packers' publicity director Chuck Lane said. "He enjoyed the role of being able to control the elements, to be in charge. In theory, that gave him control of the playing surface."

When the Cowboys arrived in Green Bay and asked to work out Saturday in Lambeau Field, Lombardi raised a fit. He said nobody could use the field because it was covered by a tarp and all lined and ready for the game, and they wouldn't have time to reline it before Sunday's game.

Jim Kenzil, second in command to Rozelle, reminded Lombardi that it was a championship game and the Cowboys darn well better use it Saturday. Kenzil said he would get guys off the street, if necessary, and with NFL personnel in town they would reline the field after the Cowboys had worked out.

"It became a shouting match," Kenzil said of his go-around with Lombardi. "Finally, I told him, 'OK, uncover half the field. To the 50.' And he said, 'I won't uncover it past the 20.'" Later, at dinner, he changed his mind. He told Kenzil that he would turn it back to the 50.

The temperature was in the teens and the wind was calm Saturday, and when the tarp was rolled back 50 yards, puffs of steam rose from the

They played a football game in 13 below zero weather, and 50,861 people in Lambeau Field tried to keep from freezing. It was the coldest New Year's Eve in the cold history of Green Bay, and everybody had good reason to warm up later.

heated field. The Cowboys were loose and happy as they went through a short workout. Bob Hayes, the team's world-class sprinter, ran a couple of deep patterns, broke a sweat, and said, "It feels good."

Lambeau Field was in relatively good condition. The heating system seemed to be paying off. "Everything's OK," Landry said.

"If we have another day like this, it will be ideal," Dallas linebacker Chuck Howley said.

Linebacker Lee Roy Caffey broke past a Dallas blocker to zero in on Don Perkins while a Packer defender grabbed the Cowboy runner from behind. Perkins rushed for 51 yards in 17 carries on the frozen turf.

Lombardi was like a little kid with an electric train as he showed off his electric blanket system to a group of writers who had been watching the Cowboys practice. He met with them in a small control room off the north tunnel of the stadium and told them how the electric coils were laid in the grid the length of the field, six inches below the surface and a foot apart, and how a thermostat controlled all of it.

In the little room with the lights blinking, he was like a mad scientist, showing writers from Dallas and New York how it worked. Some wondered if Lombardi understood one thing about it, but, by God, he thought it was working.

Green Bay linebacker Dave Robinson (No. 89) stopped Don Perkins, who had little help from Cowboy teammates, including Pettis Norman (No. 84).

Chuck Mercein, who joined the Packers after the eighth game of the season
when Lombardi ran out of running backs, broke clear for 19 yards on a short
pass from Bart Starr as Mel Renfro (No. 20) prepared to tackle him. It was a key
play in the Packers' 68-yard drive in 12 plays.

The Cowboys got on their buses and returned to the Holiday Inn in Appleton, believing that playing conditions would be quite tolerable the next day.

The next morning dawned bright and clear. The wind, as forecast, had arrived, but that wasn't the most noticeable change.

Defensive linemen Bob Lilly and George Andrie were Dallas roommates. When Lilly awoke, Andrie had already dressed and gone to an early Mass. Lilly looked out the window and couldn't believe how pretty it looked . . . so sunny and clear.

Then Andrie came back and didn't say anything about the temperature outside. He got a glass of water, pulled back the curtain and threw the water on the window. The water froze before it ran down to the windowsill.

It was 16 below zero!

"When it [the final drive] began, when we were 67 yards away or whatever it was, we were gathered together on the sidelines and someone said, 'Well, we got it.' That's all anyone said. We didn't do a lot of shooting off at the mouth."

—BOB SKORONSKI

143

Bob Skoronski, the Packers' left tackle, slept well in his Green Bay home the night before the game. He knew the temperature had plunged during the night, and all he could do was try to block out the incredible conditions outdoors.

"The game is going to be played no matter what," he said with a shrug. "We've been coached along that line all the time. We never worried about the weather."

Willie Davis was staying at the Northland Hotel downtown. During the night he heard the windows of his room rattling from the fierce wind. The next morning, he bumped into a couple of writers in the hotel lobby who had been out for breakfast, and he asked them, "Jeez, how cold is it?" They told him it was below zero.

"Had I known it was going to be that cold, I would have slept better," Davis said, hardly looking forward to what was ahead. His car, parked inside, turned over right away, and he was on his way to the stadium.

Bart Starr slept well at his west-side home and went to an early service at the First United Methodist Church in Green Bay with his dad, a Southern gentleman who was in town for the game.

"I didn't know the actual temperature at the time," Bart said. "It was so cold that neither one of us talked about it. Neither of us wanted to bring it up. All the way to church, coming back, and driving out to the stadium, not one word was said about the weather."

"Winning is not everything. It is the only thing."

—VINCE LOMBARDI

At Lambeau Field, assistant coaches Ray Wietecha and Bob Schnelker were heading back to the Packers' locker room after inspecting the field two hours before the game. As soon as the tarp was removed, it began freezing fast. They didn't have the nerve to tell Lombardi that his heating system was breaking down, so they passed along the news to Chuck Lane.

Vince Lombardi was bundled up against the incredible weather. After the game was over, he said he went for the touchdown instead of a field goal because "I didn't want all those freezing people in the stands to have to sit through sudden death."

Boyd Dowler was more than Dallas defender Mike Johnson could handle as he caught a Bart Starr pass and scored on this eight-yard play. The Packers' big flanker scored his second touchdown on a 46-yard pass from Starr as Green Bay jumped off to a 14–0 lead.

"I went in there and told him that the heating system had failed and that his field was frozen," Lane said. "He flew into a rage, acting as though I had destroyed his heating system. He went out and inspected the field, and I got away from him and went up to the press box. He was looking for someone to kill at that point, and I didn't want to be the guy.

"That was the first year they had the heated field. They never had the expertise or experience to regulate it properly. They put a tarp over the top of it, and the tarp didn't breathe, so the heat would come up underneath and form condensation, and the moisture would drip back into the field. Once they took the tarp off, it froze quickly."

Danny Villanueva waited for the ball to be placed down on a 21-yard field-goal attempt. Villanueva made the kick just before the half, and the Cowboys, who had been unable to gain more than three first downs, left the field trailing only 14–10.

John Harrington, the engineer who installed and operated the system, insisted it would work down to zero degrees. "But when the temperature dropped to 16 below and with that wind, it just couldn't hold it," he said. "We had it up as high as we dare go. We couldn't do any more."

Inside the Packers' locker room, Lombardi was trying to convince his players that they could handle bad weather better than the other team. He walked outside again, and when he came back he was very cold and kept saying, "It's our kind of day, boys, it's our kind of day."

The mental state of the Packers was summed up best by Willie Davis. "I'm thinking the Ol' Man is crazy," he said. "The question ultimately is whether anyone can survive playing in these conditions."

Chuck Mercein, who would be a last-minute starter at fullback in the place of Jim Grabowski, who reinjured his leg in the pregame warm-ups, tried running on the field and found it as hard as concrete with frozen ruts.

"All the pieces of mud you get from the field on your cleats were stuck to the surface," he said. "It was like running on a stucco wall laid flat on the ground. There were sharp clumps of dirt frozen into the ground. This is what made it so hard to run."

Normally, Davis did not wear additional clothing underneath his uniform because he felt it restricted his movement. But on this day the first thing he did was to put on long underwear that equipment manager Dad Braisher was passing out to everyone.

Gloves? "No gloves," Lombardi told everybody. So Davis had his hands taped almost the equivalent of gloves, and that's the reason he suffered frostbite—touching his taped but exposed fingertips to the frozen turf.

Starr wore a long-sleeved warm-up under his jersey and long johns down to his knees. The uniforms at that time were not equipped with a pouch so the quarterback could try to keep his hands warm between plays. He, too, would suffer frostbite in his right fingers.

The Cowboys tried to stay warm as they returned to their plastic-covered bench area equipped with space heaters. It didn't help much to relieve the discomfort of Jethro Pugh, Cornell Green, and Mike Gaechter.

Lance Rentzel was all alone as he grabbed a pass from Dan Reeves on the first play of the fourth quarter. Reeves swept to his left, drawing in the Packer defenders, and threw an option pass to the uncovered Rentzel. The play covered 50 yards and put the Cowboys ahead for the first time, 17–14.

The Cowboys came well supplied with extra sweatshirts, socks, underwear, gloves. They cut two slits down the front of Don Meredith's jersey, large enough for the quarterback to put his hands into the fleece-lined pockets of a sweatshirt.

When Jethro Pugh, the Cowboys' huge defensive tackle, left the Dallas dressing room and stabbed his cleats into the turf, he said, "That bastard Lombardi. He turned off his machine."

In the press box the windows were freezing up, making it almost impossible for the writers to see the game. Lane sent members of the press box crew to a Mobil station across the street from the stadium to buy cans of antifreeze. They squirted the antifreeze on the top of the press box windows, and when it started running down it melted the frost.

In order to provide as much protection and warmth as possible for the players, the ground crew constructed shelters around both benches. They stretched heavy tarpaulins and sheets of plastic over the top, rear, and ends

SEASON RECORD

DATE	OPPONENT	W/L	GB	OPP	LOC	ATTENDANCE
9/17/67	Detroit Lions	T	17	17	GB	50,861
9/24/67	Chicago Bears	W	13	10	GB	50,861
10/1/67	Atlanta Falcons	W	23	0	Milw	49,467
10/8/67	Detroit Lions	W	27	17	Det	57,877
10/15/67	Minnesota Vikings	L	7	10	Milw	49,601
10/22/67	New York Giants	W	48	21	NY	62,585
10/30/67	St. Louis Cardinals	W	31	23	StL	49,792
11/5/67	Baltimore Colts	L	10	13	Balt	60,238
11/12/67	Cleveland Browns	W	55	7	Milw	50,074
11/19/67	San Francisco 49ers	W	13	0	GB	50,861
11/26/67	Chicago Bears	W	17	13	Chi	47,513
12/3/67	Minnesota Vikings	W	30	27	Minn	47,693
12/9/67	Los Angeles Rams	L	24	27	LA	76,637
12/17/67	Pittsburgh Steelers	L	17	24	GB	50,861

NFL WESTERN CONFERENCE PLAYOFF

12/23/67	Los Angeles Rams	W	28	7	Milw	49,861

NFL CHAMPIONSHIP

12/31/67	Dallas Cowboys	W	32	17	GB	50,861

SUPER BOWL II

1/14/68	Oakland Raiders	W	33	14	Mia	75,546

149

of the bench areas, furnishing as much protection from the wind as possible. Several large butane heaters were placed in front of the bench areas, with blowers directing the hot air on the players' legs and feet.

Just before the kickoff, Tex Schramm stood at midfield. He looked at Lombardi, who grinned and put his hand near the field, as if it was warm. The Cowboys' GM just shook his head in dismay.

The Packers started fast. They scored the first time they had the ball. Starr directed an 82-yard drive in 16 plays, passing eight yards to Boyd Dowler for the touchdown. In the second quarter, Starr and Dowler

Bart Starr and Vince Lombardi waited on the sideline before the Packers' final drive. With 4:54 to play and trailing 17–14, the Packers marched 68 yards in 12 plays and scored with 13 seconds left. It was one of the greatest drives of all time.

connected on a 46-yard pass play and, after Don Chandler's conversion, made it 14–0. It looked like a rout in the making.

But in the second quarter, the Cowboys got one touchdown back when defensive end Willie Townes hit Starr for a big loss, forcing a fumble. George Andrie picked up the loose ball and lumbered seven yards into the Green Bay end zone. Moments later the usually sure-handed Willie Wood dropped a punt on the Green Bay 17, and Phil Clark recovered for Dallas. Danny Villanueva kicked a 21-yard field goal for the Cowboys just before the half, and the Packers left the field leading, 14–10.

The University of Wisconsin–La Crosse Marching Chiefs were the featured halftime entertainment, but their performance had to be canceled. The band had tried to practice at 10:00 in the morning and then went to the nearby Brown County Arena to warm up. Once inside, 11 members of the band needed medical attention and had to be taken to the hospital for treatment.

Meanwhile, in the Packers' locker room at halftime Lombardi was trying to get his team to settle down and play and forget about the brutally cold weather. But how could you forget it? "Frankly, it was a real problem for us," Davis said. "It had taken away some of our focus."

Neither team scored in the third quarter. But on the first play of the fourth period, the Cowboys caught the Packers' defense napping. Meredith called a running play and handed the ball to Dan Reeves, who ran to his left. When Bob Jeter and Willie Wood, the Packers' defenders on that side,

Coach Tom Landry showed little emotion as Starr scored the winning touchdown. Later, he said, "The sneak surprised me a little. If it had failed, they were lost. There's no way they could have gotten off another play."

Bob Lilly, the Cowboys' All-Pro defensive tackle, was more than happy to get dressed and out of Green Bay. Later he explained to reporters that he should have called a timeout, gone to the bench, and gotten a screwdriver so he could have dug some cleat holes in the ice to stop Bart Starr on his winning quarterback sneak.

Jerry Kramer, who threw a key block on Bart Starr's winning touchdown, explained to newsmen that it was the "biggest block I ever made in my life."

came up fast to stop the run, Reeves pulled up and fired a perfect option pass to Dallas wide receiver Lance Rentzel, who was wide open. The play covered 50 yards and put Dallas ahead for the first time, 17–14.

Shadows were creeping across the field now and the temperature was dropping. Nothing was working for the Packers. Time was running out. And blood pressures were shooting up all across Wisconsin.

After Wood returned a punt to the 32, the clock showed 4:54 to play as Starr huddled with his offense, 68 yards from the Dallas goal line. It was one of the all-time gut checks.

"I'll always remember looking in the huddle and the faces of the other players, thinking about saying something. I didn't say a word," Starr recalled. "As I looked in their eyes, I could see they were ready."

Guard Jerry Kramer thought of all the years of hard work it took the Packers to remain on top. For the first time, he had doubts about whether they could stay there.

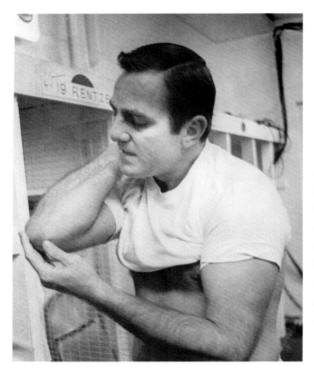

Quarterback Don Meredith of the Cowboys checked his elbow in the Dallas dressing room. Meredith, his hands numbed by the cold, completed only 10 of 25 passes for 59 yards.

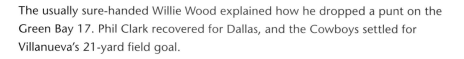

The usually sure-handed Willie Wood explained how he dropped a punt on the Green Bay 17. Phil Clark recovered for Dallas, and the Cowboys settled for Villanueva's 21-yard field goal.

"I thought, well, maybe the time has come for us to lose," he said. "But I had a second thought immediately. I thought that if we went, we'd go swinging."

This was the moment of truth for the Packers. Suddenly, everything started clicking. There were no fumbles, no dropped passes, no mistakes.

Starr, his fingers numb from the cold, completed every pass. Donny Anderson looked like Paul Hornung, and Chuck Mercein was another Jim Taylor.

There were two minutes left to play and the Packers were on the Dallas 30. For the fourth time in the drive, Starr threw to a back, and now it was Mercein—the fullback Lombardi picked up from the scrap heap when injuries depleted his corps of runners—who was coming through for him.

"I rode home with my dad after the game. He was really pumped up, more so than usual, and he told me that I had just seen him coach his next-to-last football game. I think I was one of the first people he told."

—VINCE LOMBARDI JR.

"Chuck alerted me that the Dallas linebackers were really backing off deep to try to shut off our inside routes to our wide receivers," Starr said. "So I call this particular pass. He was well open outside on a flair route."

Mercein took Starr's short pass, eluded linebacker Dave Edwards, and ran 19 yards, going out of bounds to stop the clock on the Dallas 11.

Then Starr ran a play that he called the best he ever made in a situation like this. It was called a GIVE 54—a sucker play.

Gale Gillingham, the Packers' young left guard, pulled out and ran to his right. Bob Lilly, reading a run to the right, went with him, and Starr handed the ball to his fullback. Mercein shot through the hole left by Gillingham and ran to the 3-yard line.

"All I needed to do was check with Bob Skoronski, our left tackle, and see if he could get a good block on the defensive end on his side," Starr said. "When Bob said he could, I ran it."

Still, the Dallas defense was psychological terrorism. It was like the dungeon master tightening the rack on the prisoners.

It was, well, Anderson being stopped cold on two running plays, almost fumbling on one. Sixteen seconds were left when Starr took his last time-out and went to the sideline to confer with Lombardi. A field goal that would have tied the game and sent it into sudden-death overtime was never

Hundreds of fans swarmed onto the field. They rushed toward the goal posts at each end. Dozens of men and boys were boosted up to the crossbars and uprights. The posts began to buckle and crumble. The folks of Titletown USA officially began the celebration of their third straight NFL title.

discussed. They agreed that the game should be won or lost on the next play.

Starr told Lombardi that he wanted to run the 31-wedge play, where the back goes to the hole between right guard Jerry Kramer and center Ken Bowman. He also told the coach that if the linemen could get their footing on the ice-hard surface, he would keep the ball himself and sneak in. All Lombardi said to Starr was, "Run it and let's get the hell out of here."

When Starr went back to the huddle, he did not tell anyone he was going to keep the ball. Mercein believed he was going to get it.

As Starr was calling the play, the thought crossed his mind that should Mercein slip on the icy surface, he wouldn't be able to get to the hole in time. He also thought of the time he scored a touchdown in somewhat similar conditions in a game against the San Francisco 49ers in Milwaukee County Stadium and the Packers won.

So it came down to Starr's fateful decision, called by many one of the biggest gambles in pro football history. Hand the ball to Mercein, or keep it himself?

Starr kept it. He dove his body between the fierce blocks of Kramer and Bowman and squeezed into the end zone. Right behind Starr was Mercein, who could not stop his momentum on the ice. Mercein threw his arms up, not signaling the touchdown but to show officials he didn't push Starr into the end zone, which would have been a penalty.

157

Finally, it was over. The frozen tundra boiled down to one quarterback who was dangerously sure of himself.

The Packers won, 21–17. They were NFL champions again, for an unprecedented third time in a row.

"It was a dumb call," Tom Landry said, citing the icebox circumstances and the clock all but drained. "But now it's a great play."

Look at it any way you want, but the Packers still had the Cowboys' number. They didn't so much beat the Cowboys as put them out of their misery.

Ben Wilson, a bruising 6'1", 230-pound fullback, powered his way for yardage before being tripped up by Oakland linebacker Gus Otto. A former Los Angeles Ram, Wilson had played only sparingly for the Packers in 1967 but was a surprise starter in Super Bowl II. Wilson responded by gaining 65 yards in 17 carries.

CHAPTER 7

SUPER BOWL II

On the Friday afternoon before Super Bowl II, Vince Lombardi stood in front of a crowded ballroom at the Doral Hotel in Miami Beach. He grabbed the front of the podium and stared at the assemblage of reporters sitting in front of him.

For a fleeting moment, the possibility loomed. Would Lombardi announce that this would be his last game coaching the Green Bay Packers?

It was a genuine possibility. The rumors had been circulating for weeks, months.

Lombardi opened the press conference by saying he just wanted to make one statement. "I'm real happy to be in this game. Period. That's all," he said. "Now the ball is yours, gentlemen."

The reporters fired back. They grilled him, asking him time and again if he would be back as coach of the Packers. Would he leave Green Bay? Would he stay with the Packers as general manager? Would he coach another team?

"I'm not sure I have the answer myself," he said. "This is not the proper time to make such a decision. I've got a game to play. I'm exhausted. I'm tired. It's the wrong time to make any decision."

The questions continued. How long would he need to make his decision? Days? Weeks? Months?

"Look, maybe I won't make any decision at all," the 54-year-old coach and general manager of the Packers said. "Sometimes I think you guys just want to get rid of me."

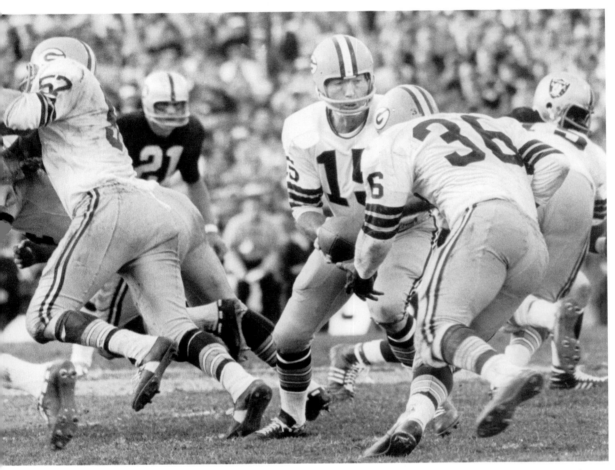

Bart Starr handed off to Ben Wilson as the Packers pounded it out against the Raiders. Although he completed 13 of 24 passes for 202 yards and one touchdown and was later named the game's most valuable player, Starr called 41 running plays as the Packers controlled the game.

The 1967 season had been an extremely difficult year for Lombardi. Without Jim Taylor, without Paul Hornung, and with Bart Starr missing four games with injuries, they finished 9–4–1. They were down to bare bones for running backs after Elijah Pitts and Jim Grabowski were lost for the season. They brought in two yard-sale fullbacks, Chuck Mercein and Ben Wilson, to fill the holes.

Then they reached deep and won two of their toughest and most meaningful games, back-to-back. They cruised to a crushing 28–7 victory over the powerful Los Angeles Rams for the Western Conference crown in Milwaukee and then rallied to get past the revengeful Dallas Cowboys, 21–17, for the NFL title in frozen Lambeau Field.

Lombardi was so sure his team would return for Super Bowl II that he told assistant coach Dave Hanner, who was on a recruiting trip for the Packers in the spring of 1967, to find a good place for the team to stay when—not if—it played in the Super Bowl in Miami. Hanner picked out the Gault Ocean Mile Hotel in Fort Lauderdale, and Lombardi booked the place nine months ahead of time.

The Oakland Raiders had won 13 games with Daryle Lamonica, the Mad Bomber, at quarterback in 1967. They had run roughshod through the American Football League, having scored 468 points and given up just 233. The Raiders routed the Houston Oilers, 40–7, for their first AFL championship.

John Rauch was the head coach. But the man totally in charge of the Silver and Black operation was dynamic Al Davis, a managing general partner and former coach. Davis was commissioner of the AFL in 1966 and had declared all-out war on the rival NFL. He wanted nothing more than to bring the NFL's almighty Packers to their knees.

"Lombardi was short with newsmen the year before in California, but he was astoundingly mellow that week in Miami. He handled one difficult situation beautifully. A Miami sportscaster grilled him relentlessly one day at a large press conference and no one quite knew what to do. The sportscaster was blind. Lombardi was gracious, brilliantly gracious, and he finally offered to see the man privately at the end of the press conference. When the conference ended Lombardi was given a warm ovation. That was a first!"

—CHUCK JOHNSON, THE MILWAUKEE JOURNAL

Davis loved being the underdog. "Imagine," he said mockingly, "the lil' ol' Raiders on the same field with the Green Bay Packers. Imagine." The Raiders arrived in Miami 10 days before the game, wearing their 14-point underdog role like a tattoo.

Meanwhile, Lombardi kept his team in its Green Bay icebox. None of the Packers appreciated the plan. Foremost among them was Ray Nitschke, who had been treated for frostbite in the Ice Bowl game.

Nitschke was told by doctors that the only way he could avoid getting frostbite again was to stay out of the cold. "How the hell do you do that, and go out and practice in five degrees?" he said as the workouts continued in Lambeau Field while the ground crew brushed off the snow.

"You go out and get up a good sweat," Lombardi said. End of conversation.

Donny Anderson found guard Jerry Kramer a perfect escort as he took off against the Raiders. He scored the Packers' second touchdown on a two-yard run.

As the game went on, Ben Wilson hunted for his contact lens on the Green Bay sideline and had plenty of help. Wilson led both teams in rushing with 65 yards.

Oakland split end Bill Miller was tripped up by Tom Brown. The Packers' safety wasn't so fortunate on another play when Miller slipped behind Brown in the end zone and Lamonica hit him with a 23-yard touchdown pass.

If Lombardi told his team to go out on the bay and work out on an ice floe, that's what it would have done. As defensive tackle Henry Jordan said, "When Vince tells me to sit down, I don't even look for a chair."

But Lombardi's plan to stay in Green Bay to get ready for a second Super Bowl performance wasn't working out too well. Weather conditions continued to be so bad after three days in Lambeau Field that he moved practice indoors to a local high school gym.

"We couldn't do much of anything because of the cramped space of that gym," Donny Anderson recalled. "We couldn't run patterns, couldn't do the things we needed to do, and he got real frustrated."

On the Sunday before the game, with the temperature seven degrees below zero, the Packers left for Miami.

This showdown with the Raiders was no grudge match, like the Cowboys. It wasn't the same. The only fear for the Packers was coming up with football's most dreaded disease—not living up to expectations.

Lombardi's message was simple before they departed. First he talked about the prestige of representing the Packers and the NFL again, emphasizing that they "damn well not let that Mickey Mouse league beat you." And then he contradicted himself and talked about how good the Raiders were.

"You better be ready or they'll knock your blocks off," he caustically warned them. "We're not going down there on vacation."

Vacation? When Lombardi finished, Jerry Kramer looked at Forrest Gregg and Gale Gillingham and said, "Can you imagine anyone fool enough to think that going anywhere with this man would be a vacation?"

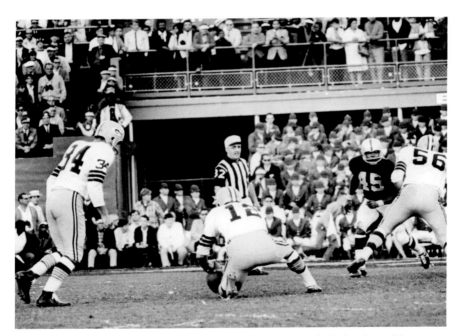

With Zeke Bratkowski holding, Don Chandler was set to kick the first of four field goals—this one from 39 yards away. His other field goals were from the 20, 43, and 31. The last one hit the crossbar and went over. He also added three conversions.

Travis Williams carried the ball on one of his eight runs against the Raiders. The Road Runner, who returned four kickoffs for touchdowns during the regular season, didn't get a chance to break one in the Super Bowl.

Maybe Lombardi was thinking of the team's last visit to the Orange Bowl. That was on January 3, 1965, and the Packers lost to the St. Louis Cardinals, 24–17, in something the NFL called the Playoff Bowl. It was a game between the league's 1964 runner-up teams, a game he had little interest in. Lombardi called it the "shit bowl."

Afterward, Lombardi moaned about "a hinky-dink football game, held in a hinky-dink town, played by hinky-dink players. That's all second place is—hinky-dink." He said that he would never come back and had no intention of ever finishing second again.

Well, here they were back in Miami as NFL champs. Warm, sun-drenched, tropical southern Florida—the prettiest place in the world with the palm trees swaying in the ocean breeze.

"What a difference," guard Fuzzy Thurston said, as the team worked out in the Fort Lauderdale ballpark the New York Yankees used in spring training.

"How sweet it is," defensive end Willie Davis added.

"Maybe my toes will thaw out," Nitschke hopefully thought.

Hobbling around on crutches as a spectator was Jim Grabowski, the injured fullback. He had undergone surgery after reinjuring his knee during the warm-ups before the Ice Bowl game and wanted to be with his teammates in Florida.

"Everyone felt like they could finally shed the winter coats," tackle Forrest Gregg said. "Everybody was kind of frisky. We had plenty of time to prepare for the Raiders."

The Packers were a tired football team as they cranked up preparations for the Raiders under the warm Florida sun. They were sluggish, but Lombardi had his way of getting their attention. It was anything but a week in heaven getting ready for the Raiders.

"It had been a tough year," Bart Starr said. "After winning two consecutive championships and going for a third, everyone in the league

---

"When we played Oakland in the Super Bowl we knew they played a lot of bump and run and we had never been exposed to that other than the Bears. So we went to Miami and the first day we got out there early. We brought out some defensive backs, we got some ends and Bart and I just stood there and threw sideline passes all day. And we kept doing it, doing it, doing it. We didn't throw a lot in that game but the ones Bart did throw were complete. That was Lombardi precision."

—ZEKE BRATKOWSKI

Daryle Lamonica wondered how he could get the Raiders back into the game. The Mad Bomber completed 15 of 34 passes for 208 yards and two touchdowns but was hounded ceaselessly and sacked three times by the Packers.

wanted a little extra piece of us. It was a very demanding season, and we had some key injuries. I was one of them. It took us a while to get up to the level we needed to be during practice."

Lombardi was a bit easier to get along with in Miami. He even broke a long-standing rule and allowed the players' wives to accompany the team to Florida. While he had been intense and difficult in preparation for the first NFL vs. AFL showdown in Los Angeles, he was more subdued in Miami.

"I'm not saying he didn't have the urgency to win. That was obvious," tackle Bob Skoronski said. "But he was more melancholy about it. He'd delve on some things more than he would have before. He was so business, so professional most of the time, and now—I don't want to say he was a more loving guy—but it was a little bit more gentle."

On Friday Lombardi broke the news to the team about his future—or tried to at a team meeting. In his book, *Instant Replay*, Jerry Kramer explained the scene:

> We had our afternoon meeting at 2:45 today, a little early, because Coach Lombardi had to go to an AFL-NFL meeting in Miami. He came into the meeting room wearing a blue shirt, a tie, dark pants and glasses.
>
> He turned and faced us. "OK, boys," he began, then stopped and rubbed his hands together for several seconds, obviously thinking about what he was going to say. "This may be the last time we'll be together, so . . . uh . . ." His lips actually began to tremble; his whole body quivered. He looked like he was about to start bawling. He never finished the sentence. He sat down, facing the movie screen, right next to the projector, his back to all the guys, and said, "Let's break up."

Kramer said the defensive players left the room, going off to their own meeting, and Lombardi stayed with the offense team without saying a word. He put on the projector and let it run, not even bothering to run the film back and forth until late in the movie.

The players were left wondering if this was the last game Lombardi would coach them. Donny Anderson and Gale Gillingham, playing their second years with the Packers, didn't know exactly what to believe. But most of the older players pretty much knew what was going to happen.

"We heard the rumors," Gregg said. "As a football player, you are accustomed to rumors. The rumors are going on all the time. This was probably the first real confirmation that he would not be back as coach.

"Everybody was kind of quiet about it. We started to whisper. Well, maybe he's not coming back. This may be his last game. It was motivation for us to win the game."

"If a man is running down the street with everything you own, you won't let him get away. That's tackling."

—VINCE LOMBARDI

This is the one thing that Al Davis feared the most. His worst scenario was for the Packers to come storming into the Orange Bowl believing they were playing their last game under Lombardi.

The Raiders were headquartered in Boca Raton. They practiced at the St. Andrew's Boys School, a private Roman Catholic institution. Close to

SUPER BOWL II
January 14, 1968

The Green Bay Packers vs. the Oakland Raiders
The Orange Bowl, Miami, Florida
Score: Green Bay 33, Oakland 14
Attendance: 75,546

SCORING SUMMARY:

Green Bay	3	13	10	7	- 33
Oakland	0	7	0	7	- 14

GB: Chandler 39-yard field goal
GB: Chandler 20-yard field goal
GB: Dowler 62-yard pass from Starr (Chandler kick)
Oak: Miller 23-yard pass from Lamonica (Blanda kick)
GB: Chandler 43-yard field goal
GB: Anderson 2-yard run (Chandler kick)
GB: Chandler 31-yard field goal
GB: Adderley 60-yard interception return (Chandler kick)
Oak: Miller 23-yard pass from Lamonica (Blanda kick)

the small football field was a swamp populated by alligators and water moccasins. After inspecting the landscape, Raiders wide receiver Fred Biletnikoff said he would not be running any sideline patterns.

The Raiders were careful to say nothing that might stir up the Packers. Daryle Lamonica talked of how Bart Starr had always been his idol. They spoke of the Packers with overstated respect but claimed to have no fear. Many of Oakland's young players recalled watching many of these same Packers on television during their junior high school days.

"It's a little like playing against your father," one of them said. "These guys were my childhood heroes."

The most interviewed Raider was Ben Davidson, a 6'7", 275-pound defensive tackle with a trademark handlebar mustache. The AFL had built up Davidson as being a wild man, a bloodthirsty savage who intimidated quarterbacks. The bigger the name, the bigger they fall, like Joe Namath, who suffered a broken cheekbone when Davidson tore into him.

Davidson started his career with the Packers when he was picked up as a free agent in 1961. He was known as Big Ben. Tick tock.

"I remembered Ben," Skoronski said. "He came to Green Bay in the middle of November wearing Bermuda shorts. He had these monstrous legs. I thought he must never get cold.

"He was seen quite often around town riding a motorcycle with his wife. They were people who did things a little different. That was OK. He was a good guy.

"He had a handlebar mustache. Someone asked me what I was going to do to him in the game, and I said I was going to trim his mustache."

The Packers respected the Raiders a lot more than they did the Chiefs, whom they had whipped, 35–10, a year ago. For one thing, Oakland had

Willie Brown and Ben Davidson (No. 83) were a couple of spent Raiders after watching the Packers build on their lead. Davidson had spent a brief period as a Packer in 1961. "I remember Ben Davidson," Bart Starr's wife, Cherry, said. "He was a very nice man and we all liked him. He didn't have a mustache then, but that doesn't matter, I guess."

Ray Nitschke, the Packers' veteran linebacker, paused in the battle to take a few calm breaths. At halftime, Nitschke and a group of older Packers got together in a corner of the locker room and vowed to play the last 30 minutes for the Old Man.

much better cornerbacks than Fred (the Hammer) Williamson and Willie Mitchell, whom Starr exploited in the Los Angeles Coliseum.

"Yes, their secondary was stronger," Starr said as he studied Oakland films.

The Raiders respected the reach of Green Bay wide receivers Boyd Dowler (6′5″) and Carroll Dale (6′2″) but thought Willie Brown and Kent McCloughan could stay with them. Brown and McCloughan were considered two of the finest cornerbacks in the AFL, and Dave Grayson and Rodger Bird were good safeties.

"We felt we could get matchups from a passing game because of our receivers," Starr said. "We also believed the strength of our offense was running the ball. So our approach was to go with our typical game plan and take advantage of certain little things."

Bart Starr handed off to Travis Williams while guard Gale Gillingham led the interference as the Packers ran the power sweep to the left.

Donny Anderson came to the Green Bay sideline after knifing through the Raiders' defense for a two-yard touchdown run. Anderson picked up 48 yards in 14 carries and caught two passes for 18 yards.

In other words, Lombardi would stick to a game plan that he had proved to be all but unstoppable for years.

Nobody gave the Raiders much of a chance. Super Bowl II was written off as a mismatch before the teams came eyeball to eyeball. *Sports Illustrated* went so far as picking the Packers to win by four touchdowns.

Nevertheless, everybody wanted to see it. The Orange Bowl filled to its 75,546 capacity in contrast to the thousands of empty seats in the Los Angeles Coliseum the previous year, and the game was carried by CBS with Ray Scott handling the play-by-play and Pat Summerall as analyst.

Just before kickoff on a 68-degree day, Lombardi made a surprise announcement. Ben Wilson would start at fullback instead of Chuck Mercein, who had started in the Packers' previous two victories over the Rams and the Cowboys.

"Five or ten minutes before the game, coach Lombardi came over and asked how I felt," Wilson said. "I told him I felt fine. He looked at me kind of funny, and walked away. A few minutes later he came back again and asked how I felt. I said 'fine.' And the coach said if I felt fine, good, then he would start me."

The pieces were now in place for the Packers to defend their Super Bowl title.

The first time the Packers got the ball, Starr methodically moved them 44 yards to the Oakland 32, and Don Chandler kicked a 39-yard field goal.

Travis Williams was a happy Packer after the game. Although he didn't have the kind of game the Packers expected of him, he was $15,000 richer and soon would be fitted with a Super Bowl ring.

There was nothing a frustrated Daryle Lamonica (left) could do but watch as Herb Adderley sped goalward with an interception and with teammate Ron Kostelnik (No. 77) in front of him. Lamonica was trying to hit Fred Biletnikoff on a quick slant, but Adderley cut in front of him, made the interception, and returned it 60 yards for a touchdown to put the game out of reach.

Midway through the first half, Starr drove them from the Green Bay 3 to the Oakland 13, and Chandler kicked another field goal, from the 20. The longest gains on those two drives were a 17-yard pass to Dale and a 14-yard run by Starr.

And then came the big play. On a play-action pass, Starr found the Raiders in the wrong defense and hit Dowler down the middle for a 62-yard touchdown.

"They blew a coverage," Dowler said later. "It wasn't a case that I just went out and beat McCloughan. I think Howard Williams was supposed to come across from safety, and he didn't do it. That's why I was wide open. It was too easy."

Down 13–0, the Raiders threw a scare into the Packers—but it was only a scare. Lamonica put together a 78-yard drive. From the Green Bay 23, wide receiver Bill Miller slipped behind safety Tom Brown and Lamonica got rid of the ball just before Willie Davis slammed into him. Miller made the catch at the 5 and ran into the end zone.

After that, the game was utterly suspenseless. It had all the excitement of a master butcher quartering a steer.

Just before the first half ended, Donny Anderson punted to Oakland's Rodger Bird, who called for a fair catch on the Raiders' 45-yard line but dropped the ball. Dick Capp, activated the day before the game by Lombardi, recovered for the Packers.

"I guess he wasn't accustomed to catching left-footed punters," Anderson said.

With six seconds left in the first half, Chandler kicked his third field goal—a 43-yarder—and the Packers had a 16–7 lead.

At halftime Lombardi kept saying that nine points isn't enough as the coaching staff went over changes he wanted. At the same time, a few of the veterans got together in the corner of the dressing room and talked about the coach.

"We decided to play the last 30 minutes for the Old Man," Jerry Kramer said. "I said I wouldn't be surprised if Lombardi retires before too long and all of us love him. We didn't want to let him down."

The Packers broke the game open in the third quarter. Starr put together the game clincher. It was third and 1 to go on the Green Bay 40. This is where No. 15 killed the Raiders.

Starr faked a handoff to Wilson going into the line and completed a pass to Max McGee, who was playing for the last time. The play covered 35 yards, and seven plays later Anderson ran the last two yards for the touchdown to give Green Bay a 23–7 lead.

177

> *"The minute the other team made a mistake—as one of the writers said— it was like bleeding in front of a shark. Tex Maule said that a team is a reflection of its head coach. I think the Packers were just that. They were very efficient, just like him."*
>
> **—CHUCK LANE**

Vince Lombardi enjoyed what he saw as the Packers poured it on the Raiders in the Orange Bowl. The Packers led 16–7 at halftime, and Lombardi kept saying nine points wasn't enough. Behind Lombardi is Phil Bengtson, the Packers' defensive coordinator. Lombardi appointed Bengtson to succeed him as head coach.

In the Orange Bowl press box, Al Davis seemed to be having as much fun as a toll collector on the Illinois Tollway.

Before the quarter was over, Chandler kicked his fourth field goal, from 31 yards. The ball hit the crossbar and went over it.

The Raiders were hanging on the ropes. One more big right would do it.

The haymaker came early in the fourth quarter. Cornerback Herb Adderley cut in front of Biletnikoff, picked off Lamonica's pass, and sprinted 60 yards for the Packers' third touchdown and a 33–7 lead. The Raiders came back with a consolation touchdown on Lamonica's 23-yard pass to Miller.

Donny Anderson drew a crowd of Oakland defenders as he broke loose. Closing in on the Packers' halfback is big Ben Davidson, the Raiders' 6'7", 275-pound defensive end.

Vince Lombardi kept a keen eye on his Packers as the game neared its end. Later, in the winners' locker room, Lombardi smiled happily and said, "It wasn't our best effort."

SEASON RECORD

DATE	OPPONENT	W/L	GB	OPP	LOC	ATTENDANCE
9/17/67	Detroit Lions	T	17	17	GB	50,861
9/24/67	Chicago Bears	W	13	10	GB	50,861
10/1/67	Atlanta Falcons	W	23	0	Milw	49,467
10/8/67	Detroit Lions	W	27	17	Det	57,877
10/15/67	Minnesota Vikings	L	7	10	Milw	49,601
10/22/67	New York Giants	W	48	21	NY	62,585
10/30/67	St. Louis Cardinals	W	31	23	StL	49,792
11/5/67	Baltimore Colts	L	10	13	Balt	60,238
11/12/67	Cleveland Browns	W	55	7	Milw	50,074
11/19/67	San Francisco 49ers	W	13	0	GB	50,861
11/26/67	Chicago Bears	W	17	13	Chi	47,513
12/3/67	Minnesota Vikings	W	30	27	Minn	47,693
12/9/67	Los Angeles Rams	L	24	27	LA	76,637
12/17/67	Pittsburgh Steelers	L	17	24	GB	50,861

NFL WESTERN CONFERENCE PLAYOFF

12/23/67	Los Angeles Rams	W	28	7	Milw	49,861

NFL CHAMPIONSHIP

12/31/67	Dallas Cowboys	W	21	17	GB	50,861

SUPER BOWL II

1/14/68	Oakland Raiders	W	33	14	Mia	75,546

The Packers' long, draining season was over. They were champions again. Lombardi was carried off the field on the shoulders of Kramer and Gregg. They, like all of the Packers, would never forget this day.

The mood in the Packers' locker room was more relief than jubilation.

"It was happy. It also was reserved," said Starr, who was named the game's most valuable player. "It was a climax to a hectic, demanding season. There was a relief that it was over more than anything."

Skoronski noticed there was a sadness about the coach. "Normally, he would have been very, very excited about winning and saying, 'We'll do it again, boys.' There was no talk like that. He was very reserved."

Lombardi again made no announcement about his future plans. Dowler wasn't convinced that Lombardi was going to quit as coach, and he dwelled on the moment of being crowned champions again.

"I thought it was a tremendous accomplishment for us to win three championships in a row," the big receiver said. "OK, what's next? I didn't think about that at all. I just thought to enjoy the moment. Here we are. We won three in a row, and nobody's ever done that. I didn't all of a sudden start pondering the future. What are we going to do without Vince?"

Nine players dressed quickly, called cabs, and headed out to the airport to catch a flight to Los Angeles. Herb Adderley, Don Chandler, Willie Davis, Boyd Dowler, Forrest Gregg, Bob Jeter, Jerry Kramer, Dave Robinson, and Willie Wood had been selected to play in the Pro Bowl. The rest of the team flew back to Green Bay.

Vince Lombardi held another Super Bowl Trophy as CBS announcer Frank Gifford and NFL Commissioner Pete Rozelle share in the presentation. After his death in 1970, the Super Bowl Trophy was renamed in Lombardi's honor.

Vince Lombardi was carried off the field on the shoulders of Forrest Gregg and Jerry Kramer after the Green Bay Packers chopped up the Oakland Raiders 33–14 in Super Bowl II. He went out a winner for the last time. Two weeks later, he resigned as coach of the Packers.

Two weeks later, Lombardi announced his long-awaited decision at the Oneida Golf and Riding Club in Green Bay. In an emotional press conference, he said he would remain as general manager of the Packers, and then he introduced the new head coach—Phil Bengtson.

If there was any resentment among the younger players that Lombardi was copping out on them, none of them said so. They wondered what it would be like without him, but—unlike fans—they understood his move.

"They said he quit because the team was getting old, and he dumped a lot of has-beens on Bengtson's lap," Donny Anderson said. "They were going around asking, 'Where is Vince's dedication now? Where is his loyalty to the Packers? Where are the sacrifice, the unity, and the discipline he preached?' I laughed at all of them, because they didn't know what they were talking about. Anybody who had been around Lombardi knew he made the only move he could possibly have made at the time."

Lombardi never interfered with Bengtson. He rarely went down to watch practice, rarely talked with players. Yet, he could not let everything go unnoticed.

"I had the distinct honor of being the only guy he chewed out that year," Anderson recalled about the first season under Bengtson. "I was going into a meeting room on a Tuesday and Vince bumped into me in the hallway and said, 'Are you ever going to learn to run that play?' He told me what I was doing wrong. He felt like I had to have an ass chewing. He was still coaching."

"After the game I walked up to him and said, 'Congratulations, Coach,' and he gave me a big hug and he said, 'Congratulations to you, too.' He was crying."

—HERB ADDERLEY

AFTERWORD

I stood on the sidelines for six of the seven games featured in this book. What a thrill it was to review all these games with the help of Bud Lea and Vern and John Biever. I'm sure you will agree they did a great job.

The 1961 Championship game was played on December 31. I was 19 years old. You can imagine what a great New Year's Eve it was for me.

The 1962 Championship game holds a number of memories for me. To return home to New York and beat the Giants a second time was a thrill. My most vivid memory was the weather. The "Ice Bowl" in 1967 has received the most attention from a weather standpoint, but in my opinion 1962 was worse. High winds, temperatures in the teens, and turf resembling a parking lot combined to make the playing conditions worse than 1967's, in my opinion. I think a number of guys who played in both games would agree.

For some reason the 1965 Championship game doesn't stick in my mind like some of the other games. I remember the sloppy playing conditions and I remember that Cleveland's great running back, Jim Brown, wasn't a factor.

I watched the 1966 Championship game against the Cowboys on TV from my home in St. Paul, Minnesota. Since I was married with children by that time, as well as working and going to law school at night, traveling to Dallas wasn't in the cards for me. My thoughts on that game are combined with the next year's game against the same Cowboys. In 1966, in the closing minutes of the game, the Cowboys had the ball on the goal line with a chance to win but failed to score when their team was called for a penalty. The next year, in a similar situation in the "Ice Bowl," the Packers had the ball on the goal line in the closing seconds of the game.

They played without a mistake, scored, and won the game. This was the hallmark of every Packer team. When the game was on the line, they produced.

Tension is what comes to mind when I recall the first Super Bowl. In the locker room before the game you could cut the tension with a knife. Some of the players will tell you they were ho-hum about the game. Don't believe it. My father was extremely tense, and most teams reflect the attitude of their coach. The fact that the Packers took an entire half to get in sync proves my point.

Enormous pressure was placed on my father and the Packers by the NFL, particularly the "old guard" owners who, at the time, carried around a lot of animosity toward the upstart AFL. The new league had cost them a lot of money as they competed with one another to sign the same players.

The 1967 Championship game sticks in everyone's mind. There were at least 500,000 people in attendance if you believe everyone who claims to have been there. With the clock ticking down and the Packers needing to drive the entire field to win the game, I started inching my way to the dressing room. It seemed obvious that we were going to lose and I figured I might as well go in and get warm. But, by golly, as the team drove steadily down the field, I started inching my way back down the sideline. What a dramatic win! As is mentioned in this book, when my father and I drove away from the stadium after the game, he turned to me and said, "You just saw me coach my next-to-last football game."

Let me add that I don't think enough has been made of the gutsy call my father made to win the "Ice Bowl." Had the Packers been stopped short of the goal line, the Cowboys would have won and you probably wouldn't be reading this book. And all the other things that flowed out of Green Bay from those years wouldn't be quite the same. A lot ended up riding on that call—certainly more than anyone realized at the time.

Super Bowl II stands out as being pretty festive. After dispatching the Chiefs the prior year, there wasn't much doubt that the Packers would win. My strongest memory is of having my nose stuck in law books for most of the time I was in Miami.

—Vince Lombardi Jr.
Bellevue, Washington

INDEX

Numbers in *italic* type refer to photographs.

193